Discovering
SPANISH
with

Walt Disney

HARRAP

PLANNED AND PRODUCED BY
BOOKMAKER

EDITORIAL DIRECTION
Marie Garagnoux • Patrick Michel-Dansac
WITH
Françoise Avril

COMPILED BY
Bookmaker

TRANSLATION
Elida Mannevy • Maggie Doyle

COLOURS BY
Jean-Pierre Sachse

LAYOUT
Design:
Claudine Roy
Produced by:
Michèle Andrault • Monique Michel-Dansac

OTHERS CONTRIBUTORS
Sylvie Decaux • Dominique Bluher • Brian Mott •
Béatrice Leroy • Christine Ehm • Régine Ferrandis •
Mathilde Kemula • Soledad San Miguel • Catherine Chevalot

PRODUCTION
Véronique Celton

TYPESETTING AND COLOUR SEPARATION
Charente Photogravure

First published by
HARRAP BOOKS Ltd, Chelsea House,
26 Market Square, Bromley, Kent BR1 1NA

ISBN 0 245-60380-8

Note to the reader

Mickey, Donald and all their pals are about to help you discover the Spanish language.

You can follow their adventures in the cartoon strips found throughout this book which will introduce you to spoken Spanish. On each page, one of the cartoons has been enlarged and changed (you can have fun spotting the differences) ; the key words to remember are grouped around the big picture.

Before setting off in your friends' footsteps, read the instructions on page 5 carefully. The guide on page 4 is intended in particular for your parents and teachers.

Foreword

Discovering Spanish with Walt Disney is a vocabulary book for 8 to 13-year-olds, whether beginners or more advanced learners. It includes 1000 words from all grammatical categories (nouns, verbs, adjectives, adverbs, etc.) which have been selected by a team of language teaching specialists. The words, and the sentences in which they appear, correspond to the recommended contents of school curricula. The selection also takes into account the interests and everyday life of children in the 8 to 13 age group.

Each page of the book has been designed to further the joint goals of teaching a basic vocabulary and introducing common expressions : there is a large drawing illustrating the words to be learnt, and a comic strip showing idiomatic phrases in the speech bubbles.

This work is a practical tool which offers the young reader a set of useful guidelines :

• Organisation by areas of meaning puts each new word into a specific context, at once linguistic and visual, revealing its meaning in relation to associated words.

• In the vocabulary pages, the reader discovers original illustrations from the Walt Disney Studios including his or her favourite characters. The authors paid special attention to the quality of the artwork, legibility and careful selection of information.

• Essential basic information such as conjugations, numbers, days and months, etc., are given in separate appendices.

• Two bilingual indexes at the back of the book make up a complete dictionary of its words, and pronunciation is given using international phonetic transcription.

The Walt Disney characters bring their own humour and appeal to this book, which is intended to be, above all, a way to learn Spanish vocabulary and have fun at the same time.

How to use this book

This vocabulary book includes 1000 words, broken down into 10 chapters, each with its own special theme. To learn words about a specific subject, just turn to the relevant chapter about that theme. The chapters go from pages 7 to 93 :

The subjects in each chapter are listed on the first page of the chapter. For example, this is the list of subjects on page 7, which is the first page of the chapter on "the house" : the garden, the house, in the house, the sitting room, the bedroom, in bed, the kitchen, the bathroom.

These subjects are illustrated by a large picture surrounded by Spanish words and sentences and their translations.

Under the illustration, a comic strip presents dialogues : the Spanish text comes in the speech bubbles, the translation below.

All the vocabulary words are given in alphabetical order in the two indexes (on pages 101 to 111), along with their translation. If you need the exact translation of a word, simply use the indexes as if you were looking the words up in a dictionary.

You will also find the conjugation tables, the lists of numbers, days and months, as well as phonetics symbols on pages 95 to 99.

la casa • the house

el jardín • the garden

Planta un árbol.
He is planting a tree.

el rastrillo
rake

la regadera
watering can

la pala
shovel

el seto
hedge

el césped
lawn

el cortacésped
lawn mower

la alameda
path

Juanito riega las flores.
Huey is watering the flowers.

Es la primavera, están en el jardín.
It is springtime; they are in the garden.

– 'Bye Donald! See you soon!
– 'Bye Daisy!

– Donald

– She loves me… She loves me not…
She loves me…
– She loves me not!

la casa • the house

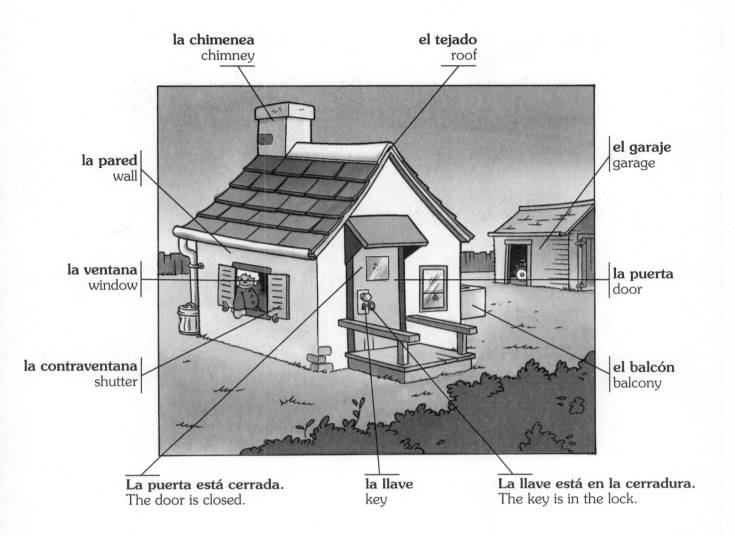

la chimenea
chimney

el tejado
roof

la pared
wall

el garaje
garage

la ventana
window

la puerta
door

la contraventana
shutter

el balcón
balcony

La puerta está cerrada.
The door is closed.

la llave
key

La llave está en la cerradura.
The key is in the lock.

Donald no puede vivir en esa casa.
Donald cannot live in this house.

– What a lovely house!
– For rent

– You want to rent a house?
I can sell you one for only $150.
– Impossible! You can't buy
a house for that price!

– You don't
believe me?
Here's the deed!

– I'll take it!

– Doll's house
– For rent

en la casa • in the house

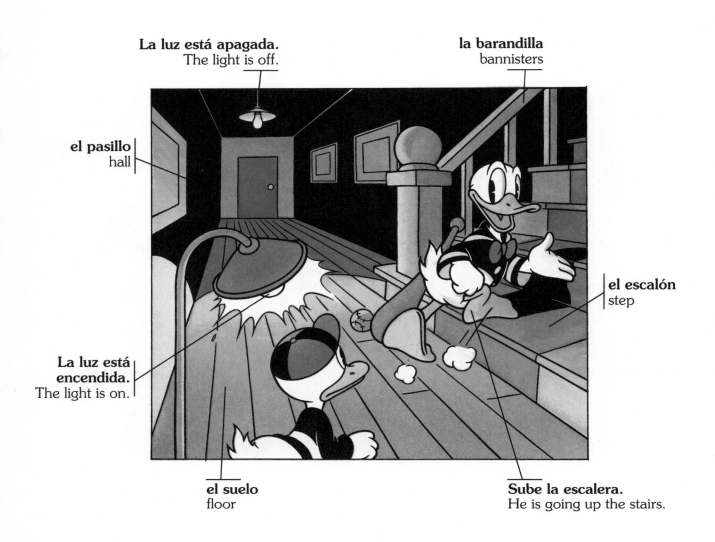

La luz está apagada.
The light is off.

la barandilla
bannisters

el pasillo
hall

el escalón
step

La luz está encendida.
The light is on.

el suelo
floor

Sube la escalera.
He is going up the stairs.

El pasillo es estrecho y oscuro.
The hall is narrow and dark.

– We're afraid…
– … it's too…
– … dark up there…

– Don't be frightened! Watch me!

el cuarto de estar • the sitting-room

Donald está leyendo un libro.
Donald is reading a book.

el florero
vase

la televisión
television

el sillón
armchair

el acuario
fish bowl

**el equipo
estereofónico**
stereo

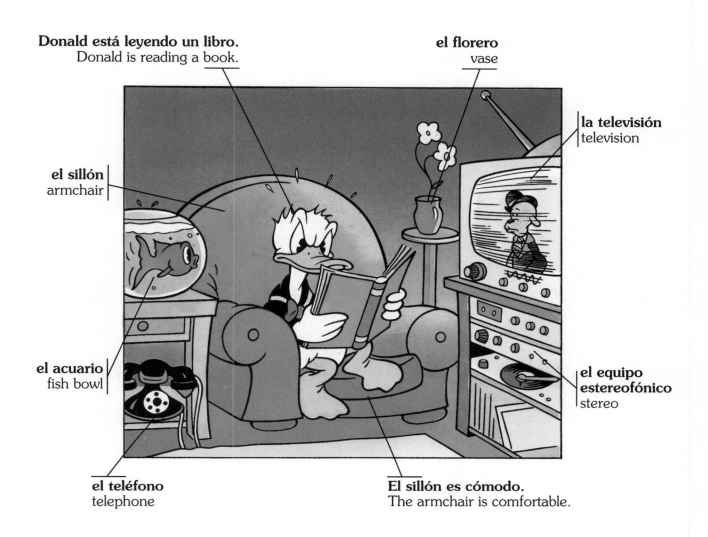

el teléfono
telephone

El sillón es cómodo.
The armchair is comfortable.

Donald está sentado.
Donald is sitting down.

¡ El pez está mirando la televisión !
The goldfish is watching television!

That fish is driving me mad! — Stop staring at me!

la habitación • the bedroom

Suena el despertador.
The alarm-clock is ringing.

la lámpara
lamp

el armario
wardrobe

la manta
blanket

el despertador
alarm-clock

la sábana
sheet

la mesilla
bedside table

el colchón
mattress

la alfombra
rug

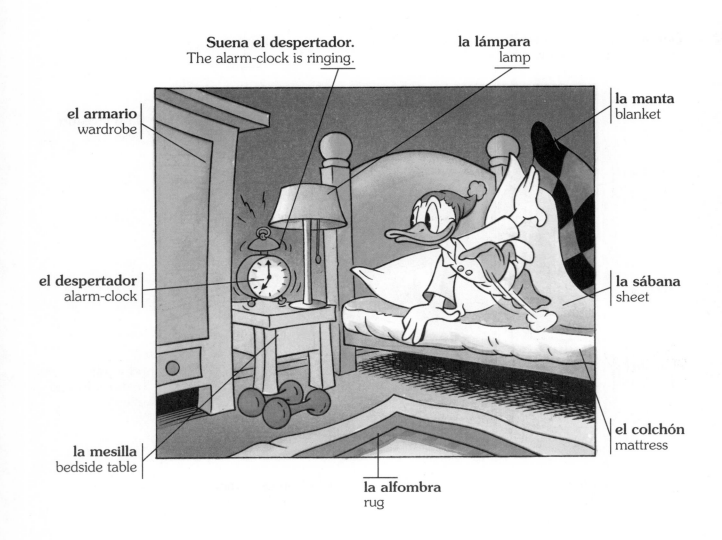

Donald se levanta.
Donald is getting up.

Pronto irá a acostarse de nuevo.
He will go back to bed soon.

– It's time!

– A little exercise…

– … to wake me up…   – Uh!

a la cama • in bed

Donald está cansado, bosteza.
Donald is tired; he is yawning.

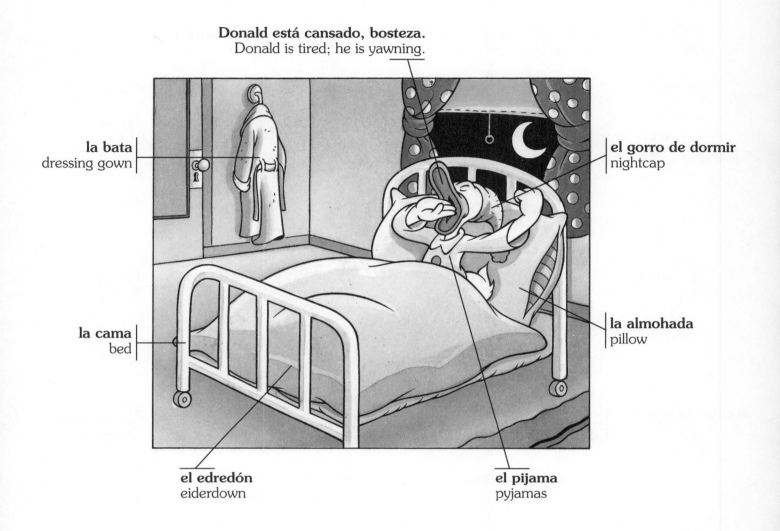

la bata
dressing gown

el gorro de dormir
nightcap

la almohada
pillow

la cama
bed

el edredón
eiderdown

el pijama
pyjamas

Es tarde, es de noche.
It is late; it is nighttime.

Se va a dormir.
He is going to sleep.

Get out of here, you horrible beast!
t me get some sleep!

la cocina • the kitchen

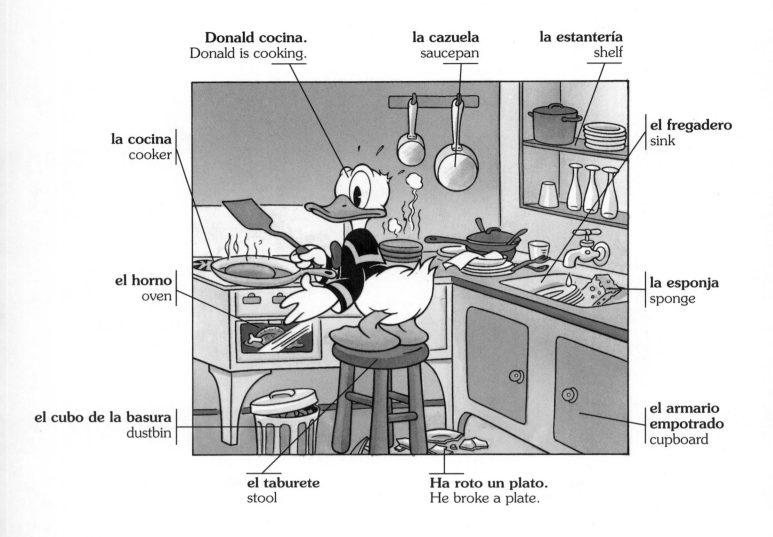

Donald cocina.
Donald is cooking.

la cazuela
saucepan

la estantería
shelf

la cocina
cooker

el fregadero
sink

el horno
oven

la esponja
sponge

el cubo de la basura
dustbin

el armario empotrado
cupboard

el taburete
stool

Ha roto un plato.
He broke a plate.

Se han colocado los vasos en la estantería.
The glasses are kept on the shelf.

No se han fregado los platos.
The dishes are not done.

– It's time…
– … to take our…
– … medicine, Uncle Donald.

– What a pleasant surprise… no one is making a face!
– Yum!

– 'Bye!
– 'Bye! This cake will taste better with some cream…

– Ugh!… Ah!

el cuarto de baño • the bathroom

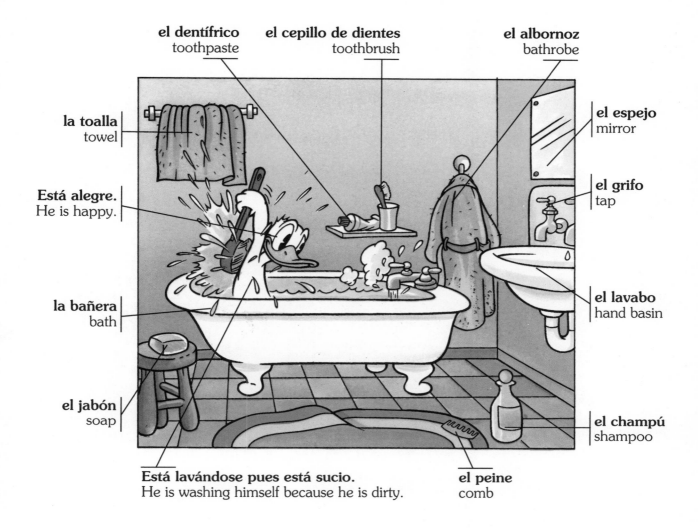

el dentífrico
toothpaste

el cepillo de dientes
toothbrush

el albornoz
bathrobe

la toalla
towel

el espejo
mirror

Está alegre.
He is happy.

el grifo
tap

la bañera
bath

el lavabo
hand basin

el jabón
soap

el champú
shampoo

Está lavándose pues está sucio.
He is washing himself because he is dirty.

el peine
comb

Donald es limpio ; toma un baño.
Donald is clean; he is having a bath.

Se cepilla los dientes dos veces al día.
He brushes his teeth twice a day.

– ZZZZ!

– ZZZZ!

la ciudad • the town

la calle • the street

el edificio
building

el semáforo
traffic light

la acera
pavement

el coche
car

el policía
policeman

el cruce
crossroads

Donald pregunta su camino al policía.
Donald is asking the policeman for directions.

Le indica el camino.
He is showing him the way.

¡ No hay atasco !
There is no traffic jam!

Está prohibido cruzar cuando el semáforo está en verde.
It is forbidden to cross when the light is green.

– No parking

– Car Park

– Post office
– Postmen's bicycles only

el tráfico • traffic

el peatón
pedestrian

Los coches tocan el claxon.
The cars are hooting.

la cabina telefónica
phone box

el faro
headlight

**Está llamando
por teléfono.**
He is making
a telephone call.

la bici
bike

Cruza la calle.
He is crossing
the street.

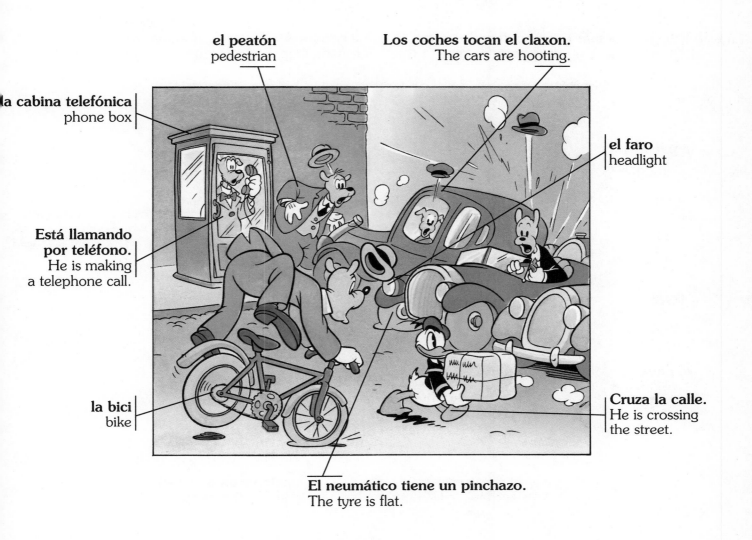

El neumático tiene un pinchazo.
The tyre is flat.

Donald ha provocado un atasco.
Donald has caused a traffic jam.

Hace creer que hay dinamita en el paquete.
He gets them to think there is dynamite in the parcel.

– There's only
one way out…

– Danger Dynamite

las tiendas • shops

En esta calle no hay más que una panadería.
There is only one bakery on this street.

la carnicería
butcher's shop

la tienda de ultramarinos
grocer's shop

la panadería
bakery

Esta tienda está cerrada.
This shop is closed.

el panadero
baker

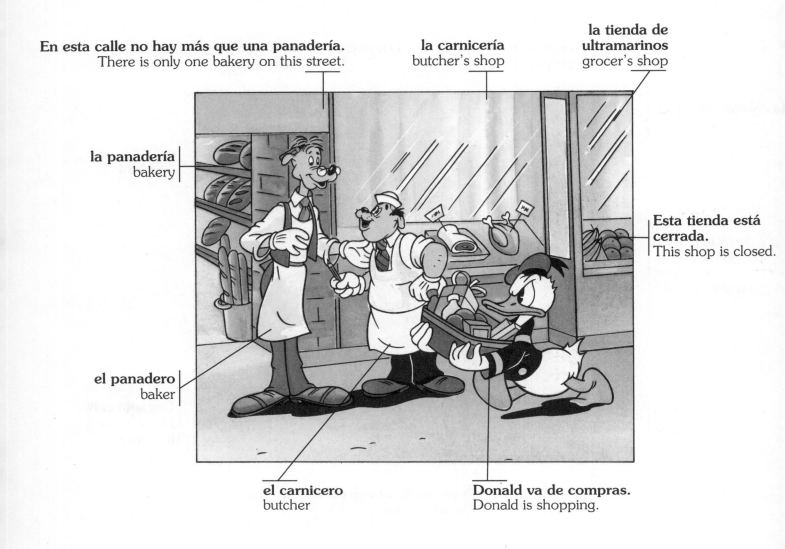

el carnicero
butcher

Donald va de compras.
Donald is shopping.

Hay muchas tiendas en esta calle.
There are a lot of shops in this street.

A Donald no le gusta ir al supermercado.
Donald does not like going to the supermarket.

– This chicken weighs two kilos.
– I'm going to check!
– Stuffed chicken

– Butcher's
– Opening hours

– Don't be offended! I just wanted to be sure.

– If you didn't shoot it…
– … why is there buckshot…
– … in the stuffing?

20

el dinero • money

Vende un sello a Donald.
He is selling Donald a stamp.

el vendedor
salesperson

el billete
bank note

el mostrador
counter

la cajera
cashier

la cartera
wallet

la moneda
coin

Paga a la cajera.
She is paying the cashier.

el monedero
purse

la caja
cash register

Donald compra un sello.
Donald is buying a stamp.

La leche está cara, el azúcar está barato.
The milk is expensive, the sugar is cheap.

May I have a two cent stamp?

– Your change!

en la estación • at the station

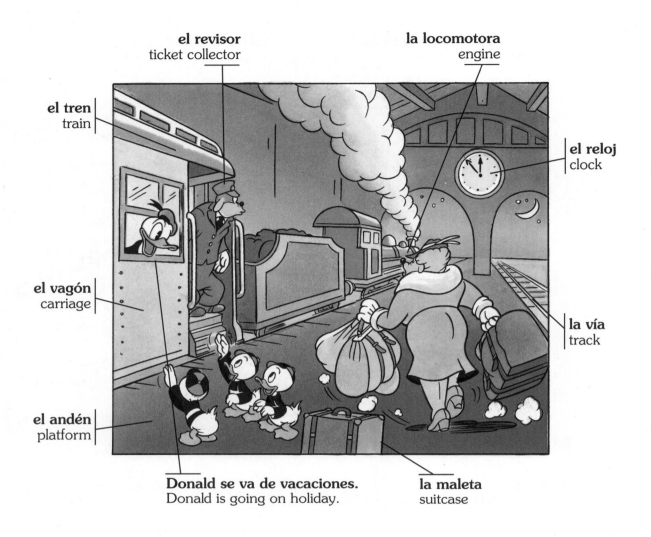

el revisor
ticket collector

la locomotora
engine

el tren
train

el reloj
clock

el vagón
carriage

la vía
track

el andén
platform

Donald se va de vacaciones.
Donald is going on holiday.

la maleta
suitcase

La señora se da prisa, lleva retraso.
The woman is in a hurry; she is late.

Su equipaje es pesado.
Her luggage is heavy.

¡HASTA PRONTO! ¡ADIÓS... TÍO... DONALD!

– See you soon!
– 'Bye...
– Uncle...
– Donald!

¡HE OLVIDADO LA MALETA!

– I've forgotten my suitcase!

¡DEPRISA! ¡EL TREN ARRANCA!

– Quick! The train is leaving!

los medios de transporte • transport

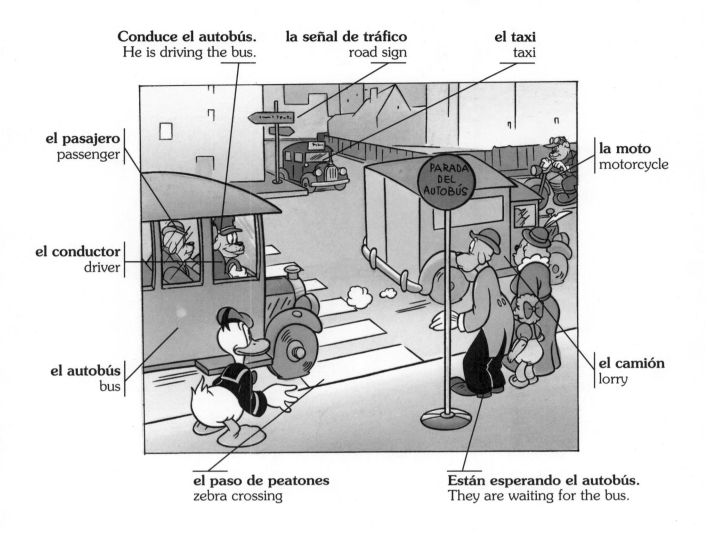

Conduce el autobús.
He is driving the bus.

la señal de tráfico
road sign

el taxi
taxi

el pasajero
passenger

la moto
motorcycle

el conductor
driver

el autobús
bus

el camión
lorry

el paso de peatones
zebra crossing

Están esperando el autobús.
They are waiting for the bus.

La señal indica las direcciones.
The road sign gives the directions.

La niña está entre el señor y la señora.
The little girl is between the gentleman and the lady.

Bus stop

– Bus stop

– Bus stop

la escuela • the school

el aula • the classroom

Es el mejor alumno de la clase.
He is top of the class.

Está borrando la pizarra.
She is cleaning the blackboard.

la pizarra
blackboard

la alumna
pupil

la maestra
schoolteacher

Pasa la página.
She is turning
the page.

el despacho
desk

la página
page

el alumno
pupil

Está escribiendo.
He is writing.

Los alumnos están en el aula.
The pupils are in the classroom.

Los alumnos trabajan bien.
The pupils are working hard.

– I'm going to see the headmaster and find out
how Li'l Davy's doing at school…

– Thank you for your help… school is an
excellent influence on Li'l Davy!
– Well…

– I don't know if school has influenced Li'l Davy, but Li'l
Davy has influenced the school!

el recreo • playtime

El profesor vigila el patio.
The teacher is watching the playground.

Corre.
He is running.

Los niños bailan en corro.
The children are dancing in a ring.

Juega a las canicas.
He is playing marbles.

Miguelito ha puesto sus libros en el suelo.
Morty has put his books on the ground.

Es un amigo de Miguelito.
He is Morty's friend.

Es la hora del recreo.
It is playtime.

Los niños se divierten.
The children are having fun.

So… You're the new kid?

– That's right! Any more questions?

– What did you learn at school today, Morty?
– That you can't go by appearances!

el cálculo • arithmetic

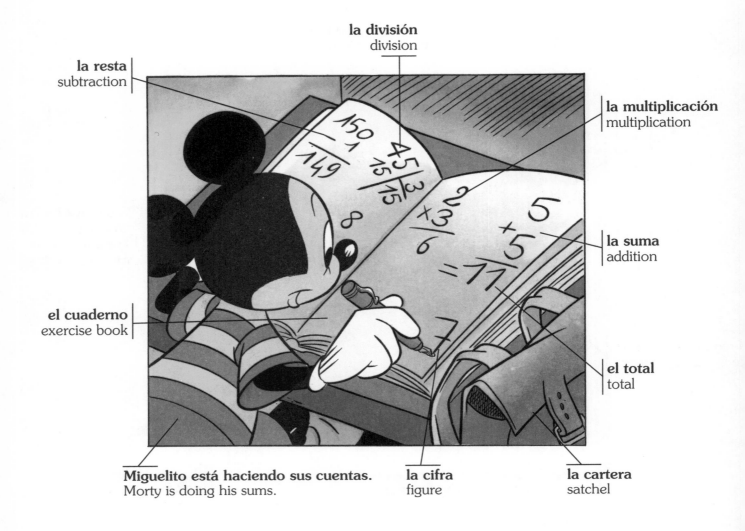

la división
division

la resta
subtraction

la multiplicación
multiplication

la suma
addition

el cuaderno
exercise book

el total
total

Miguelito está haciendo sus cuentas.
Morty is doing his sums.

la cifra
figure

la cartera
satchel

Se ha equivocado en una operación.
He has made a mistake in one sum.

– Do you want me to help you with your homework?
– X has three dollars pocket money per week.

– Bus fare, pens, sweets, a film a week… X can't do it!
– That's what I thought!

– Thanks for the raise, Mickey!

los colores • colours

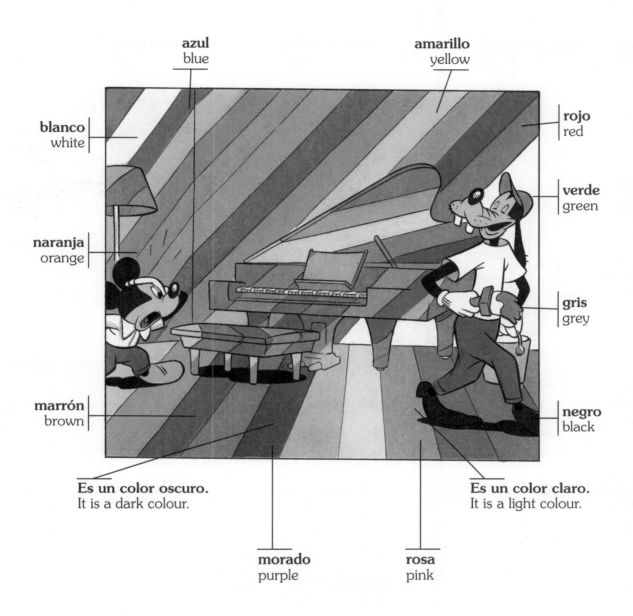

azul
blue

amarillo
yellow

blanco
white

rojo
red

verde
green

naranja
orange

gris
grey

marrón
brown

negro
black

Es un color oscuro.
It is a dark colour.

Es un color claro.
It is a light colour.

morado
purple

rosa
pink

– Good luck! I hope you'll do a good job!
– What do you mean by that? I paint the best stripes in town!

– Later…
– I don't know why, but I always worry when he does a job for me…

– You said you wanted a good job done… Well, here it is!

las formas • shapes

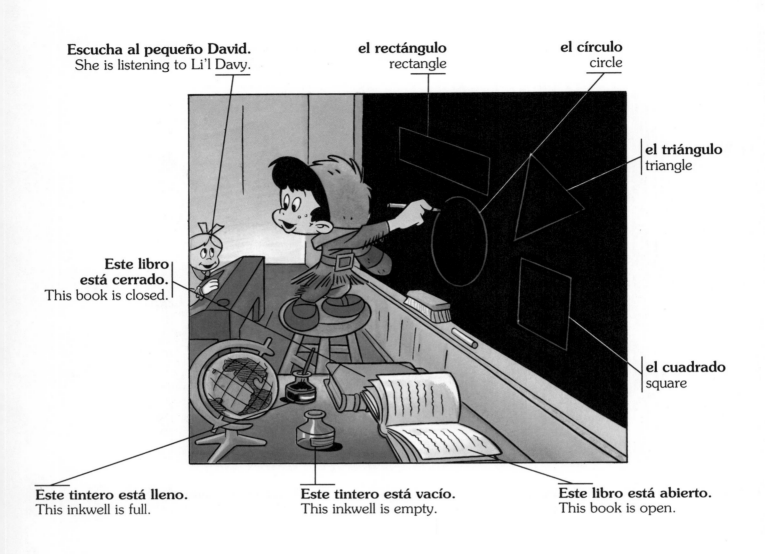

Escucha al pequeño David.
She is listening to Li'l Davy.

el rectángulo
rectangle

el círculo
circle

el triángulo
triangle

Este libro está cerrado.
This book is closed.

el cuadrado
square

Este tintero está lleno.
This inkwell is full.

Este tintero está vacío.
This inkwell is empty.

Este libro está abierto.
This book is open.

El mapamundi es redondo.
The globe is round.

ESTOY VERDADERAMENTE CONTENTO DE QUE EL PEQUEÑO DAVID VAYA A LA ESCUELA.

– I'm so happy Li'l Davy's going to school!

POR FIN VA A APRENDER ALGO...

– At last he's going to learn something…

AQUÍ TIENEN LA HUELLA DE UNA PATA DE OSO... ¿HAN ENTENDIDO TODOS BIEN?

– And this is a bear track… Has everyone understood?

la hora • time

Esta aguja marca los minutos.
This hand shows the minutes.

Esta aguja marca las horas.
This hand shows the hours.

El reloj de cuco está a la hora.
The cuckoo clock is on time.

El reloj de Goofy va atrasado.
Goofy's watch is slow.

el reloj
watch

el despertador
alarm clock

El despertador va adelantado.
The alarm clock is fast.

Esta aguja marca los segundos.
This hand shows the seconds.

Mickey da cuerda al despertador ; mañana por la mañana tocará las ocho.
Mickey is winding the alarm clock; it will go off tomorrow morning at eight o'clock.

– Sale
What a lovely cuckoo clock! I'm so happy I bought it!
Good luck!

– Now, what time is it?

– It's two o'clock! My cuckoo clock is ringing!

la gente · people

la familia • the family

Es la abuela de Ana.
She is Ann's grandmother.

Es el tío de Ana.
He is Ann's uncle.

Es el hijo de Miguel.
He is Michael's son.

Es el abuelo de Felipe.
He is Philip's grandfather.

Es el padre de Felipe.
He is Philip's father.

Son hermanos.
They are brother and sister.

Es la madre de Marcos.
She is Mark's mother.

Es la prima de Ana.
She is Ann's cousin.

Es la tía de Ana.
She is Ann's aunt.

Es la hija de Miguel.
She is Michael's daughter.

Es el primo de Ana.
He is Ann's cousin.

MIGUEL

ANA

MARGARITA

MARCOS y MARIA

Miguel es el marido de Margarita.
Michael is Margaret's husband.

Margarita es la mujer de Miguel.
Margaret is Michael's wife.

– See that? She cleans up really well!
– What a mess!

– Crash!

– I never thought you could be afraid of my family…

las personas • people

la mujer
woman

Es feliz.
He is happy.

Es joven.
She is young.

el hombre
man

la niña
girl

el nene
baby

El pequeño David es un muchacho.
Li'l Davy is a boy.

La madre lleva a su nene en brazos.
The mother is holding her baby in her arms.

Tiene dos hijos.
She has two children.

You think you can do it?
Of course! Come and get him in half an hour.

– I'm warning you…
– Now… Now…

– But… But…
– I hate getting my hair cut!

el aspecto físico · appearance

Es viejo.
He is old.

Es gordo.
He is fat.

Es feo.
He is ugly.

Es alto.
He is tall.

Es delgado.
He is thin.

Es fuerte.
He is strong.

Es bajo.
He is small.

Dingo es más alto que Mickey.
Goofy is taller than Mickey.

Mickey es más pequeño que Dingo.
Mickey is smaller than Goofy.

Juan es más gordo que Dingo.
John is fatter than Goofy.

– Mickey, do you need an orange squeezer?
– Oh yes, thanks!

– An orange squeezer would be very useful.

– That's really nice of you, Mickey! My cousin was out of work!

los cabellos • hair

Tiene el pelo corto.
He has short hair.

la cola de caballo
ponytail

el flequillo
fringe

el bigote
moustache

Es rubia.
She is blonde.

Es moreno.
He is dark.

la trenza
plait

la barba
beard

el pasador
slide

Es barbudo y tiene el pelo lacio.
He has a beard and straight hair.

La niña es pelirroja.
The little girl is red-haired.

Tiene el pelo largo.
She has long hair.

¿MICKEY, PUEDES IR A BUSCAR LA "CANGURO" DE MI SOBRINA?

SÍ...

Mickey, could you pick up my
niece's babysitter?
Yes...

¿NO LE MOLESTA QUE LLEVE MIS DISCOS?

– You don't mind if I bring my records?

VOY A DETENERLES, ¡TIENEN UNA PINTA MUY RARA!

Distributed by King Features Syndicate

– I'm going to get them to pull over; they look suspicious!

la personalidad • personality

Mickey se sorprende.
Mickey is surprised.

Pequeño David está bien educado.
Li'l Davy is polite.

Goofy está contento.
Goofy is happy.

Es famosa.
She is famous.

Goofy es pobre.
Goofy is poor.

Miss Latour es rica.
Miss Latour is rich.

¡ Mickey es amable !
Mickey is nice!

– I'm going hunting!
– OK! But don't bring back an Indian chief or a bear like you usually do…

– Go ahead and laugh, but he often can give you a nasty surprise!

– Later
– I hope you don't mind… I invited…
– No! Certainly not!

– I'm really sorry, Miss Latour!
– It's all right, Li'l Davy!
– I should have kept my mouth shut…

la ropa (1) • clothes (1)

la blusa
blouse

Lleva un vestido largo muy bonito.
She is wearing a lovely evening dress.

la corbata de pajarita
bow tie

la chaqueta
jacket

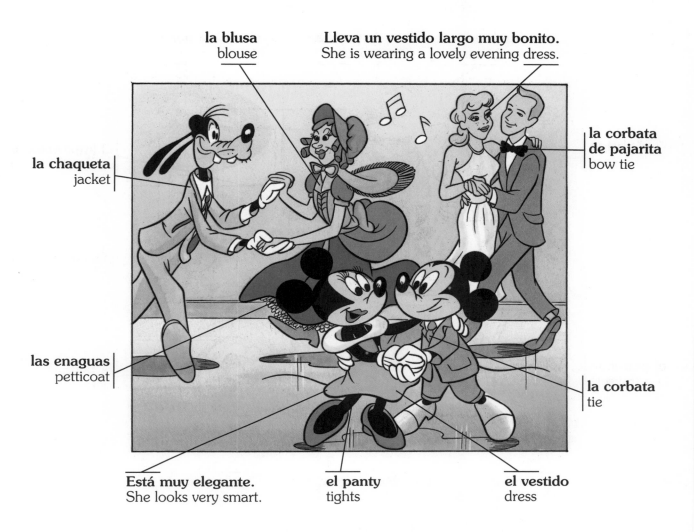

las enaguas
petticoat

la corbata
tie

Está muy elegante.
She looks very smart.

el panty
tights

el vestido
dress

Minnie se ha maquillado.
Minnie is wearing make-up.

Mickey tiene un traje nuevo.
Mickey has a new suit.

– Are you going to the dance tonight?
– No, unless I find an old-fashioned girl.

– Did Goofy find a girl he liked?

– Yes! He never does things by halves!

la ropa (2) • clothes (2)

el sombrero
hat

la percha
coatstand

la gorra
cap

el abrigo
coat

el impermeable
raincoat

el pantalón
trousers

la falda
skirt

Su americana es demasiado ancha.
His jacket is too big.

el tejano
jeans

El pantalón de Mickey es demasiado corto.
Mickey's trousers are too short.

Minnie se va a vestir.
Minnie is going to get dressed.

– You're really going to wear those this evening?
– Yes! Bullfighter trousers are all the rage now.

– That evening…
– My first guest… I hope it's Mickey!

– Here we are!

la ropa (3) • clothes (3)

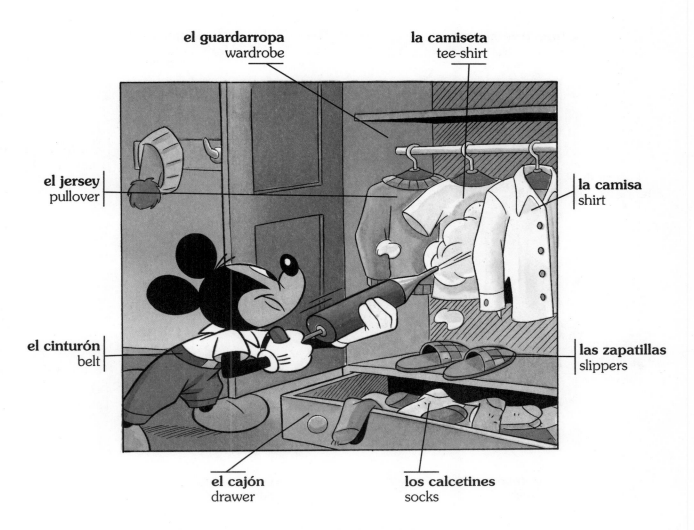

el guardarropa
wardrobe

la camiseta
tee-shirt

el jersey
pullover

la camisa
shirt

el cinturón
belt

las zapatillas
slippers

el cajón
drawer

los calcetines
socks

Hay mucha ropa en el guardarropa.
There are a lot of clothes in the wardrobe.

Ha colgado su gorro en el perchero.
He has hung his cap on the peg.

GRACIAS A ESTE PRODUCTO NO HABRÁ YA MÁS POLILLAS...

– Thanks to this spray, there'll be no more moths…

NO SABEN LO QUE LES ESPERA...

– They'll never know what hit them…

MÁS TARDE...

¡HABÍA OLVIDADO MI MEJOR TRAJE!

– Later…
– I've forgotten my best suit!

el calzado • shoes

Su bota está agujereada.
There is a hole in his boot.

Le duele el pie.
His foot hurts.

el tenis
tennis shoe

la bota
boot

el cordón
shoelace

el botín
ankle boot

el tacón
heel

el escarpín
court shoe

Los zapatos de Goofy son demasiado grandes.
Goofy's shoes are too big.

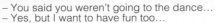

– You said you weren't going to the dance…
– Yes, but I want to have fun too…

– That's strange…
– What's it to you?

– I couldn't stand people stepping on my feet anymore.

las joyas • jewellery

la sortija
ring

Este anillo de oro brilla.
This gold ring glitters.

el pendiente
earring

la esmeralda
emerald

la perla
bead

el collar
necklace

la pulsera
bracelet

El collar de Minnie se ha roto.
Minnie's necklace broke.

el broche
brooch

el rubí
ruby

Las perlas han rodado por el suelo.
The beads rolled on the floor.

Las esmeraldas y los rubíes son piedras preciosas.
Emeralds and rubies are precious stones.

- Mickey! My beads…!
- I'll pick them up for you!

– Gosh! There are a lot of them!

– There… I think I've got them all…

– Everyone else went home long ago!

el cuerpo humano · the human body

las partes del cuerpo (1) • parts of the body (1)

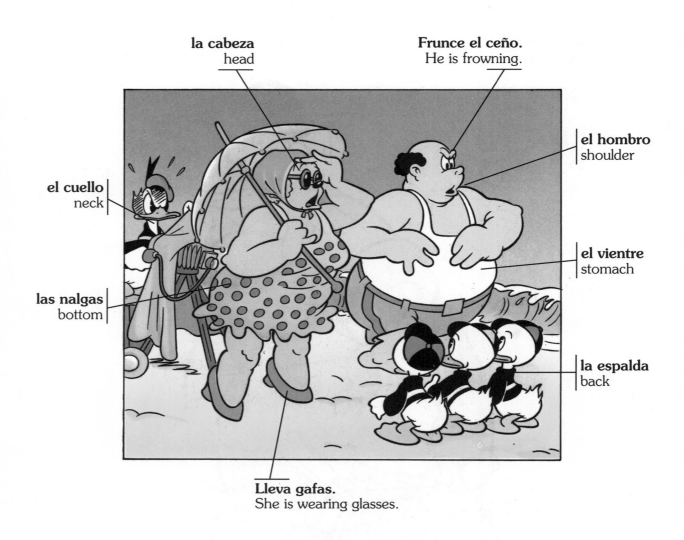

la cabeza
head

Frunce el ceño.
He is frowning.

el cuello
neck

las nalgas
bottom

el hombro
shoulder

el vientre
stomach

la espalda
back

Lleva gafas.
She is wearing glasses.

La señora da la espalda a Donald.
The lady is turning her back on Donald.

– Hey, you! Can't you see I'm taking a photo?

– Oh, Oscar!

las partes del cuerpo (2) • parts of the body (2)

Cruza los brazos.
His arms are crossed.

El masajista está de pie.
The masseur is standing up.

la pierna
leg

el brazo
arm

el dedo
finger

el pie
foot

el codo
elbow

Lleva sandalias.
e is wearing sandals.

la mano
hand

el dedo del pie
toe

la rodilla
knee

Donald está tumbado.
Donald is lying down.

El masajista tiene los brazos musculosos.
The masseur's arms are well-muscled.

A Donald le dan masajes una vez por semana.
Donald has a massage once a week.

iploma

– Crack

¡ES UN DÓLAR, SEÑOR!

– That'll be one dollar, sir!

la cara • the face

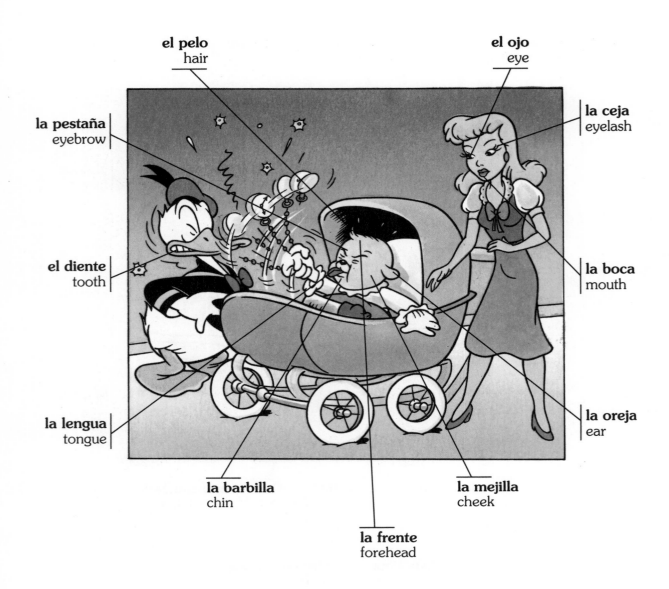

el pelo
hair

el ojo
eye

la pestaña
eyebrow

la ceja
eyelash

el diente
tooth

la boca
mouth

la lengua
tongue

la oreja
ear

la barbilla
chin

la mejilla
cheek

la frente
forehead

El nene saca la lengua.
The baby is sticking out his tongue.

– Oh! Aren't you cute!
Cootchy, cootchy coo!

– Shh!
– Boohoo!

– Look! The watch is
going tick-tock!

la salud • health

La enfermera le va a cuidar.
The nurse is going to look after him.

Le duele la cabeza.
He has a headache.

El médico está preocupado.
The doctor is worried.

la jeringuilla
syringe

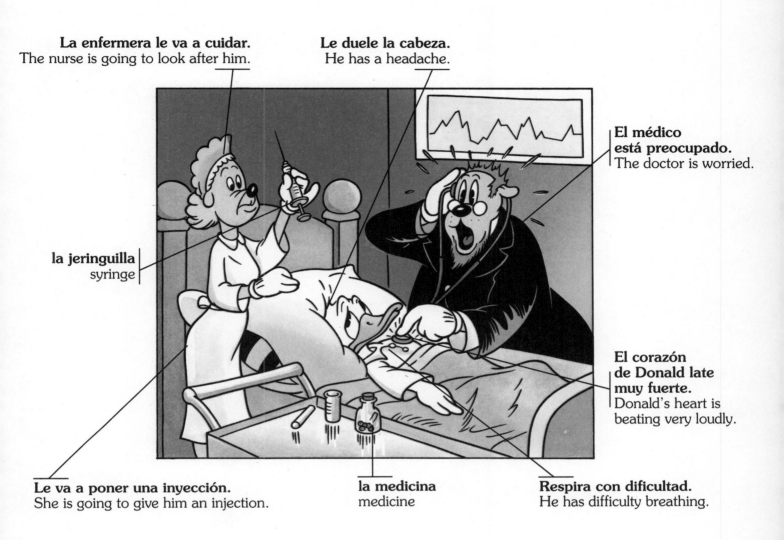

El corazón de Donald late muy fuerte.
Donald's heart is beating very loudly.

Le va a poner una inyección.
She is going to give him an injection.

la medicina
medicine

Respira con dificultad.
He has difficulty breathing.

Le han trasladado al hospital en ambulancia.
He was brought to the hospital by ambulance.

Tal vez Donald se muera.
Perhaps Donald will die.

– I'll pretend to be sick…

– Tick tock

– Ha ha! That fooled him!

– Ambulance

la comida • food

las hortalizas • vegetables

la calabaza
pumpkin

la zanahoria
carrot

la lechuga
lettuce

el guisante
pea

el pimiento
sweet pepper

el puerro
leek

la cebolla
onion

la judía verde
green bean

la col
cabbage

la patata
potato

el rábano
radish

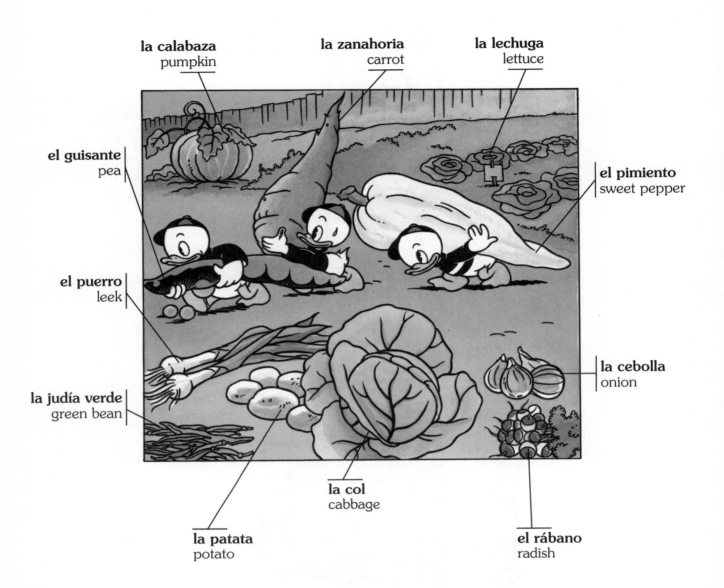

– We bought some…
– … magic fertilizer.
– Magic fertilizer
– You know, it's rain and work that make plants grow…

– It's raining! I bet everything will have grown by tomorrow!

– Morning
– I can't wait to see…

– There! I told you everything would have…
– … grown!

52

la **fruta** • fruit

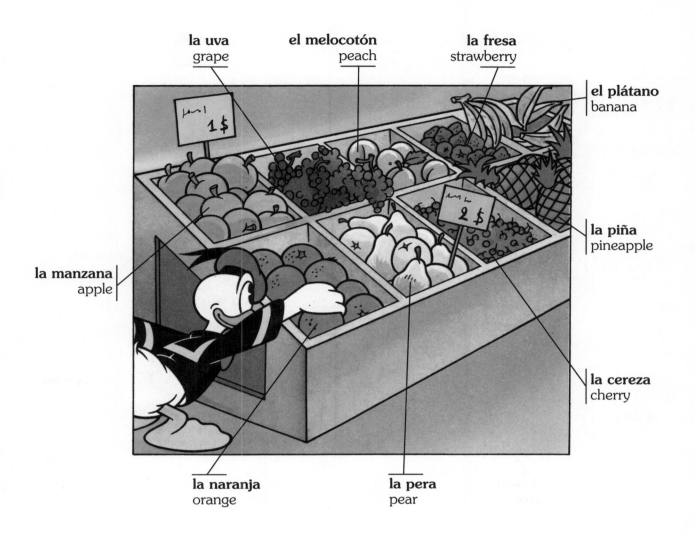

la uva
grape

el melocotón
peach

la fresa
strawberry

el plátano
banana

la manzana
apple

la piña
pineapple

la cereza
cherry

la naranja
orange

la pera
pear

Las frutas están maduras.
The fruit is ripe.

El melocotón es una fruta.
A peach is a piece of fruit.

Have you seen the lovely fruit?

– Do you want
any more?

la mesa • the table

la sal
salt

la pimienta
pepper

la silla
chair

la servilleta
napkin

el cuchillo
knife

la cuchara
spoon

el tenedor
fork

el vaso
glass

el plato
plate

Donald trae una fuente.
Donald is holding a dish.

Narciso Bello tiene siempre hambre y sed.
Gladstone is always hungry and thirsty.

– There! I hope that's enough!

– Oh dear! He's so greedy!
I hope he leaves me something
to eat…

– What? There's nothing left but the…

– … bones?

el desayuno • breakfast

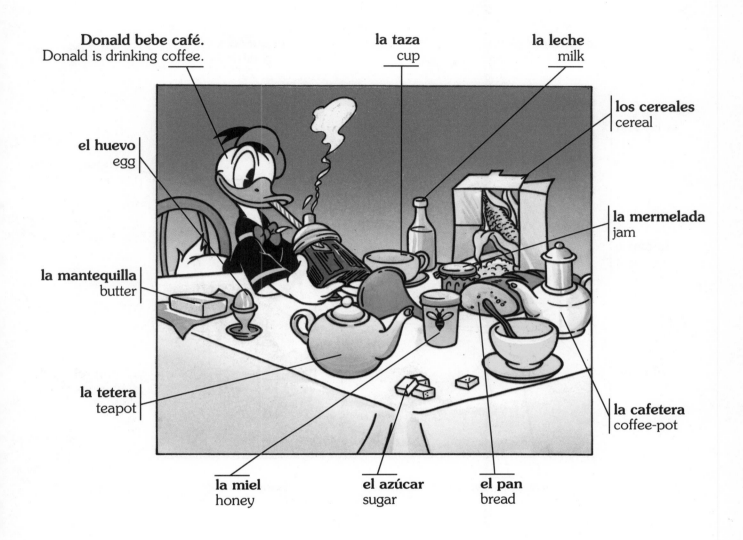

Donald bebe café.
Donald is drinking coffee.

la taza
cup

la leche
milk

los cereales
cereal

el huevo
egg

la mermelada
jam

la mantequilla
butter

la tetera
teapot

la cafetera
coffee-pot

la miel
honey

el azúcar
sugar

el pan
bread

Ha preparado el té.
He has got tea ready.

Los sobrinos no se han levantado todavía.
The nephews are not up yet.

This coffee has no sugar in it…

– This sugar dispenser really isn't very practical…

– I've a solution!

el almuerzo • lunch

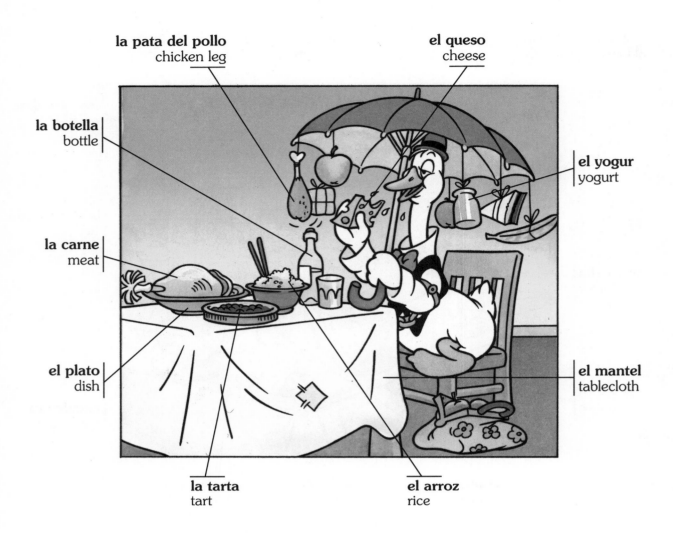

la pata del pollo
chicken leg

el queso
cheese

la botella
bottle

el yogur
yogurt

la carne
meat

el plato
dish

el mantel
tablecloth

la tarta
tart

el arroz
rice

Narciso Bello come mucho.
Gladstone eats a lot.

El queso es delicioso.
The cheese is delicious.

¡YA LO VES QUE NO HAY NADA QUE COMER!

– You see? There's nothing to eat!

¡SE LO HA CREIDO! ¡VA A VOLVER A SU CASA!

Copr | by Walt Disney Enterprises
1918 | World rights reserved

– It worked! He's going back to his house!

¡BUM!

– Plop!

la cena • dinner

**Narciso Bello ha vaciado todo
lo que había en la nevera.**
Gladstone has emptied the fridge.

**La sopa
está quemando.**
The soup
is boiling hot.

la sopera
soup tureen

onald está furioso.
Donald is angry.

el cucharón
ladle

el agua
water

la sopa
soup

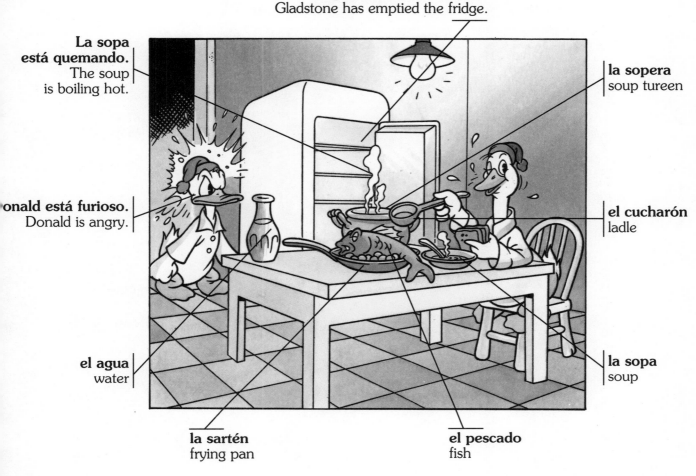

la sartén
frying pan

el pescado
fish

¡ Narciso Bello no es un verdadero sonámbulo !
Gladstone is not a real sleepwalker!

Le gusta el pescado.
He likes fish.

Where is he going?

– Into the kitchen?

la naturaleza • nature

el bosque • the forest

el nido
nest

la rama
branch

la hoja
leaf

el árbol
tree

Caen las hojas.
The leaves are falling

el tronco
trunk

la ardilla
squirrel

la castaña
chestnut

la hierba
grass

Mickey ha recogido setas.
Mickey has been picking mushrooms.

Es el otoño.
It is autumn.

Están en un claro del bosque.
They are in a clearing.

– What will we eat today, boys?
– How about an eagle-egg omelet?
– An eagle-egg omelet?

– It's delicious! And I know just where to
find the eggs in the forest!

– A little later…
– Don't wait for me! I may be a little late!

la montaña • the mountains

la gamuza
chamois

la montaña
mountain

la cumbre
peak

el águila
eagle

el corzo
deer

el chalet
chalet

Goofy está detrás de Mickey.
Goofy is behind Mickey.

el camino
track

el torrente
mountain stream

Mickey está delante de Goofy.
Mickey is in front of Goofy.

El valle está abajo.
The valley is below.

La cumbre está arriba.
The peak is above.

– It's fun collecting birds' eggs for the museum...
– Let's keep in touch on the walkie-talkie!

– Later...
– Bzzz Bzzz
– I wonder what Goofy wants...

– Have you found anything?
– No, I'm the one who's been found!

el campo • the countryside

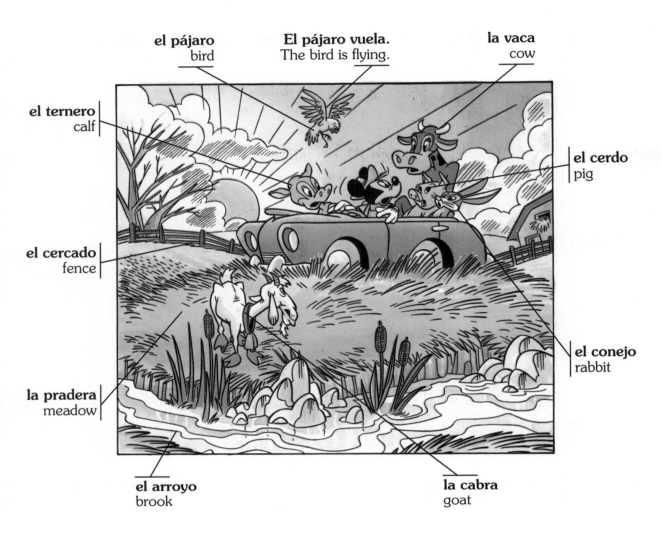

el pájaro
bird

El pájaro vuela.
The bird is flying.

la vaca
cow

el ternero
calf

el cerdo
pig

el cercado
fence

el conejo
rabbit

la pradera
meadow

el arroyo
brook

la cabra
goat

Sale el sol : es muy temprano.
The sun is rising: it is very early.

¡ Qué paisaje más hermoso !
What a beautiful landscape!

– It's too dangerous to drive in this fog! I'll pull over and wait.

– Morning...
– I fell asleep! At last the fog's lifted...

– One thing is certain, it was very foggy!

las flores • flowers

la rosa
rose

el clavel
carnation

el ramo
bouquet

el tulipán
tulip

la abeja
bee

el tallo
stem

¡ Qué bien huele !
What a lovely smell!

Esta flor está marchita.
This flower has wilted.

los pétalos
petals

la margarita
daisy

Sólo hay flores, no hay plantas de interior.
There are only flowers here; there are no green plants.

– Oh! I'm sorry!
– Florist

– Minnie, just let me explain!

el río • the river

la caña de pescar
fishing rod

el pez
fish

la orilla
bank

el pescador
fisherman

el abeto
fir tree

el guijarro
pebble

el puente
bridge

Ha pescado un gran pez.
He caught a fine fish.

la canoa
canoe

El río es profundo.
The river is deep.

El río fluye bajo el puente.
The water is flowing under the bridge.

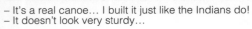

– It's a real canoe… I built it just like the Indians do!
– It doesn't look very sturdy…

– We're sinking!
– No we aren't! In a minute, we'll be in the middle of the river!

– Come back, Goofy! Come back!

el mar • the sea

el ancla
anchor

el buque
ship

el faro
lighthouse

Hace esquí náutico.
He is water-skiing.

la escollera
jetty

el barco
boat

Está nadando.
He is swimming.

Hay un buque en el puerto.
There is a ship in the harbour.

Sopla el viento.
The wind is blowing.

Get the sail down! There's too much wind!
I'm trying!

– Mickey!
– I can't do it!

– Police
– I don't suppose you'd be interested in an explanation…

el cielo • the sky

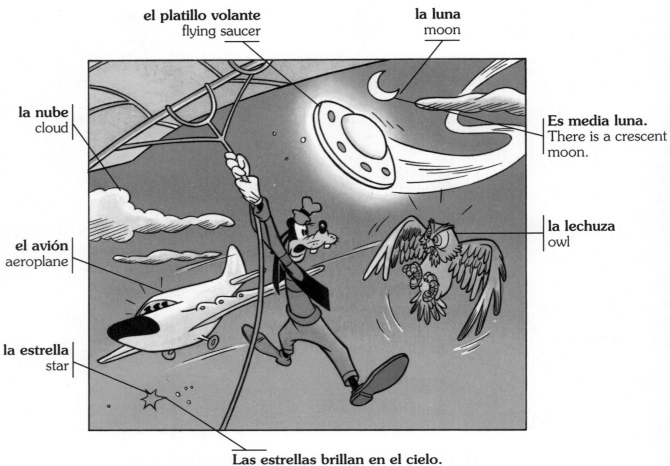

el platillo volante
flying saucer

la luna
moon

la nube
cloud

Es media luna.
There is a crescent moon.

el avión
aeroplane

la lechuza
owl

la estrella
star

Las estrellas brillan en el cielo.
The stars are shining in the sky.

El platillo volante vuela por los aires.
The flying saucer is crossing the sky.

La noche está agitada.
It is a hectic night.

– I've got an idea! I'm going to make my kite just like a seagull!
– I see…

– There we are! I'm flying away like a… Aaah!

– OK, now explain how I get back down!

la tormenta • the storm

Goofy se pone a cubierto al interior de la casa.
Goofy is sheltering inside the house.

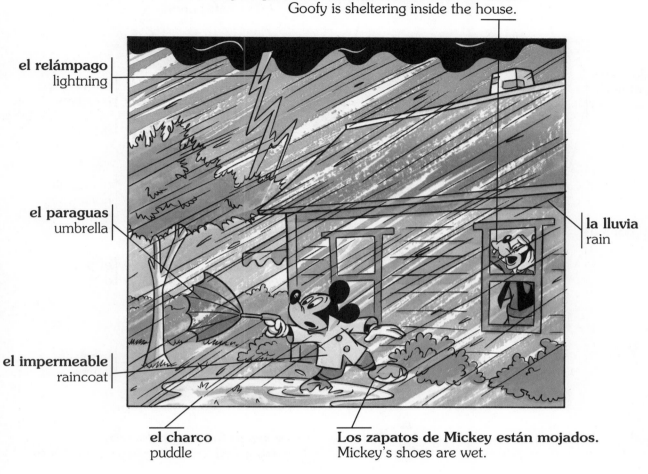

el relámpago
lightning

el paraguas
umbrella

el impermeable
raincoat

el charco
puddle

la lluvia
rain

Los zapatos de Mickey están mojados.
Mickey's shoes are wet.

¡ Hace viento !
It is windy!

Se oye el trueno.
Thunder can be heard.

I'm going to hang up my barometer and see
what the weather will be… Oops!

– It's stuck!
– Fine
– Rain

– I think I did something silly…

la granja • the farm

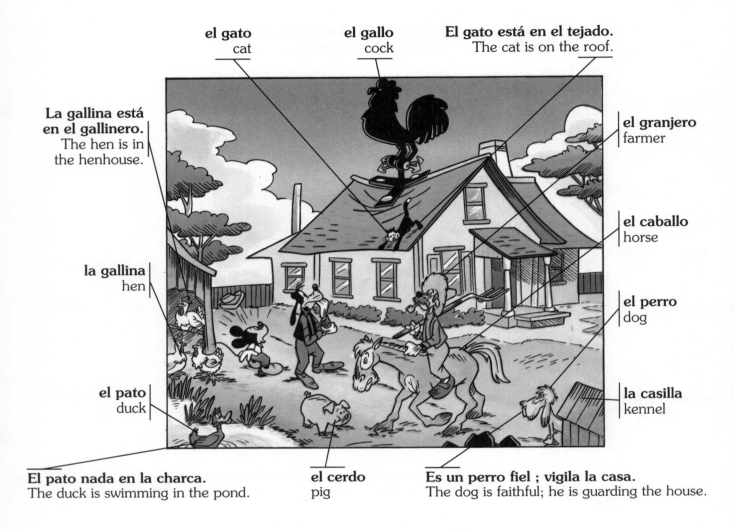

el gato
cat

el gallo
cock

El gato está en el tejado.
The cat is on the roof.

La gallina está en el gallinero.
The hen is in the henhouse.

el granjero
farmer

el caballo
horse

la gallina
hen

el perro
dog

el pato
duck

la casilla
kennel

El pato nada en la charca.
The duck is swimming in the pond.

el cerdo
pig

Es un perro fiel ; vigila la casa.
The dog is faithful; he is guarding the house.

¿ Cuántos animales hay ?
How many animals are there?

El granjero monta a caballo.
The farmer is riding his horse.

– I've decided to put a weathercock on my roof!
– That's a good idea!

– A few days later…
– I'm going to see Goofy… His weathercock must be ready by now…

– I think I must have got the instructions wrong…

los animales salvajes • wild animals

la jirafa
giraffe

el hipopótamo
hippopotamus

el mono
monkey

La cebra corre deprisa.
The zebra is running quickly.

el elefante
elephant

Mickey tiene miedo a los animales salvajes.
Mickey is afraid of wild animals.

el león
lion

la serpiente
snake

el cocodrilo
crocodile

¡ Cuidado ! El león parece peligroso.
Watch out! The lion looks cross.

La jirafa tiene el cuello largo.
The giraffe has a long neck.

PERO BUENO, MINNIE... NO HE PEDIDO QUE EMPAPELEN MI SALÓN.

¡ PERO VEN A VER QUÉ SORPRENDENTES SON ESTOS NUEVOS PAPELES !

¡MIRA! ¡PARECE UN JARDÍN DE VERDAD! ¿ TE GUSTA ?

SÍ... HE ESTADO A PUNTO DE EQUIVOCARME...

¡ESPERA A VER LO QUE YO HE ESCOGIDO PARA TU SALÓN !...

MÁS TARDE

WALT DISNEY 9-24

– But, Minnie… I didn't want my sitting-room papered.
– Come and see how amazing these new wallpapers are!

– See! It looks like a real garden! Do you like it?
– Yes… I almost thought…

– Wait and see what I have chosen for your sitting-room!…

– Later

69

el ocio • leisure

el aeropuerto • the airport

Llegadas
Arrivals

Este avión despega.
This plane is taking off.

Salidas
Departures

el avión
aeroplane

el hangar
hangar

Este avión aterriza.
This plane is landing.

la azafata
air hostess

el aduanero
customs officer

la aduana
customs

LLEGADAS

SALIDAS

ADUANA

Una señora presenta su pasaporte al aduanero.
A woman is showing her passport to the customs officer.

HOY, VAS A HACER EL ATERRIZAJE...

PUES... PUES...

10-14

¡ESTÁ BIEN! ¡AHORA, VE DESPACITO!

¡BRAVO! ¡YO NO LO HUBIERA HECHO MEJOR!

¡SOCORRO!

– You can land the plane today…
– But… But…

– That's it! Go easy now!

– Bravo! I couldn't have done better!
– Help!

la playa • the beach

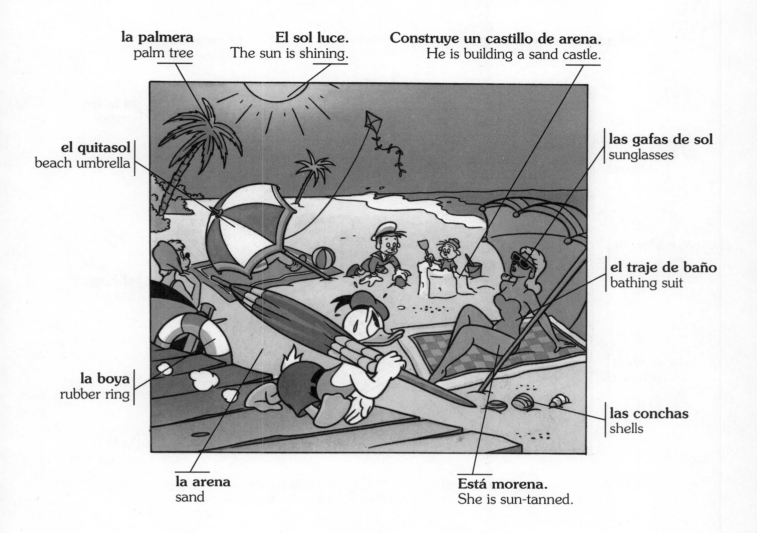

la palmera
palm tree

El sol luce.
The sun is shining.

Construye un castillo de arena.
He is building a sand castle.

el quitasol
beach umbrella

las gafas de sol
sunglasses

el traje de baño
bathing suit

la boya
rubber ring

la arena
sand

las conchas
shells

Está morena.
She is sun-tanned.

Están de vacaciones.
They are on holiday.

Hace buen tiempo, es verano.
The weather is fine; it is summer.

here're a lot of people here!…   – Where can I sit?

el camping • camping

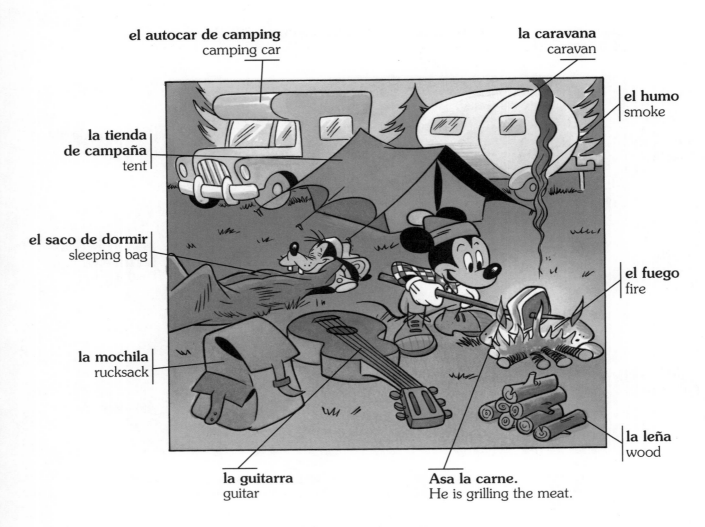

el autocar de camping
camping car

la caravana
caravan

el humo
smoke

la tienda
de campaña
tent

el saco de dormir
sleeping bag

la mochila
rucksack

el fuego
fire

la leña
wood

la guitarra
guitar

Asa la carne.
He is grilling the meat.

Mickey se calienta cerca del fuego.
Mickey is warming himself beside the fire.

A Mickey le encanta ir de camping.
Mickey loves camping.

– Well, Goofy, are you glad you slept in the great outdoors?
– Yes…

– Luckily, I had my sleeping bag to keep me warm!
– Yes… It was cold last night…

– Very cold!

los juguetes y los juegos • toys and games

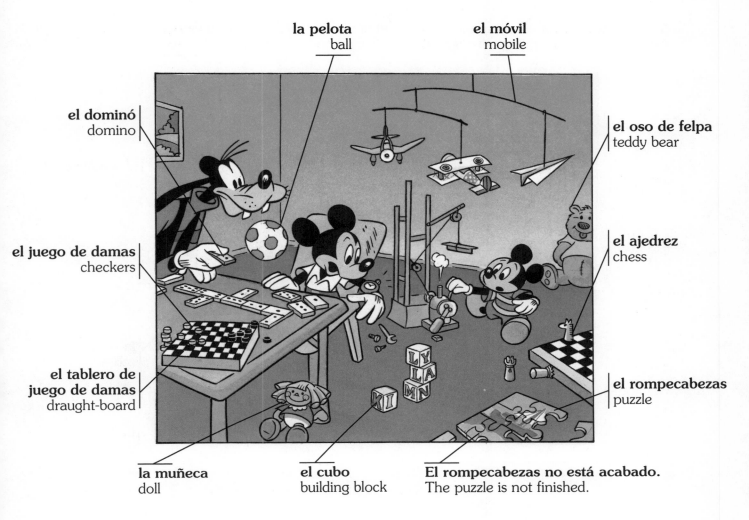

la pelota
ball

el móvil
mobile

el dominó
domino

el oso de felpa
teddy bear

el juego de damas
checkers

el ajedrez
chess

el tablero de juego de damas
draught-board

el rompecabezas
puzzle

la muñeca
doll

el cubo
building block

El rompecabezas no está acabado.
The puzzle is not finished.

En la sala de juego hay desorden.
The playroom is untidy.

La muñeca se llama Carolina.
The doll's name is Caroline.

¡VAMOS MORTY, A LA CAMA!

¡YO QUIERO JUGAR TODAVÍA, MICKEY!

– Come on, Morty! It's bedtime!
– I want to keep playing, Mickey!

¡ALE! ¡VETE A ACOSTAR!

¡YO ME DIVERTÍA MUCHO CON VOSOTROS!

– You go to bed!
– I was having such fun with you!

¡ESTA PARTIDA DE DOMINÓS ME ABURRÍA! ¡PREFIERO LOS JUGUETES DE MORTY!

¡YO TAMBIÉN!

– This game of dominos was so boring! I prefer Morty's toys!
– Me too!

el parque zoológico • the zoo

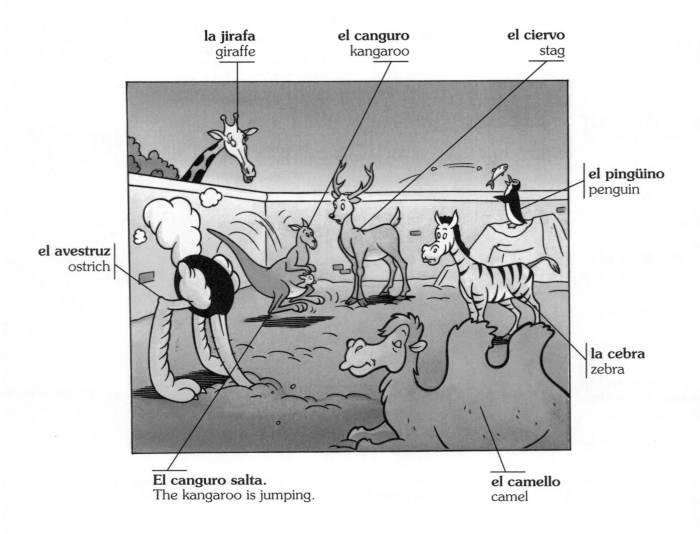

la jirafa
giraffe

el canguro
kangaroo

el ciervo
stag

el pingüino
penguin

el avestruz
ostrich

la cebra
zebra

El canguro salta.
The kangaroo is jumping.

el camello
camel

El pingüino coge un pez.
The penguin is catching a fish.

La avestruz se esconde.
The ostrich is hiding.

– What are you talking about? My ostrich is a bad influence on the other animals?

– O.K. I'll go to the zoo and see what's happening.

la pintura • painting

el lápiz
pencil

la regla
ruler

la goma
rubber

¡ Ese cuadro es una obra maestra !
This painting is a masterpiece!

Hay manchas de pintura en su delantal.
There are paint stains on his smock.

la paleta
palette

la tela
canvas

el tubo de pintura
tube of paint

el papel
paper

el pincel
paint brush

El artista pinta bien.
The artist paints well.

Ha hecho el retrato de Donald.
He has painted Donald's portrait.

It's really not expensive…
I've got to eat! I'm a poor starving
tist!
Portraits painted $ 2

la música • music

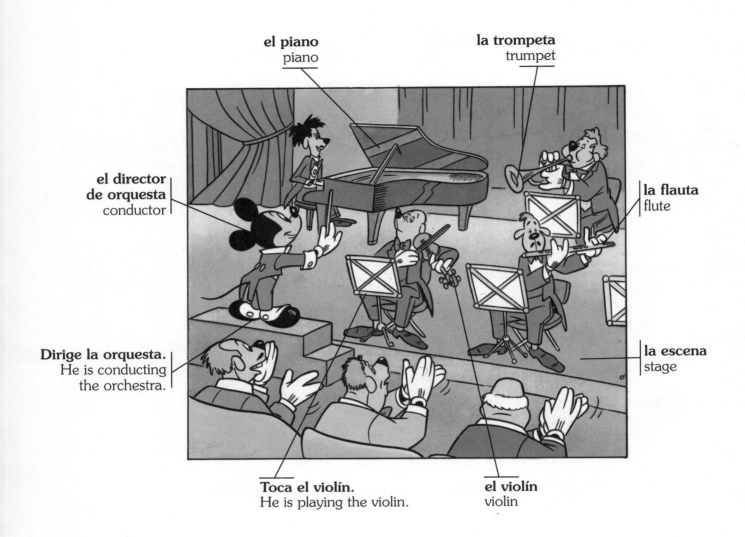

el piano
piano

la trompeta
trumpet

el director
de orquesta
conductor

la flauta
flute

Dirige la orquesta.
He is conducting
the orchestra.

la escena
stage

Toca el violín.
He is playing the violin.

el violín
violin

El público aplaude.
The audience is clapping.

– I didn't know you were giving a concert here.
– Oh really?
– Stage door

el concierto • the concert

Es un buen músico.
He is a good musician.

el saxofón
saxophone

el micrófono
microphone

el sintetizador
synthesizer

el cantante
singer

la guitarra eléctrica
electric guitar

la batería
drums

Desafina.
He is singing out of tune.

Toda la gente baila.
Everybody is dancing.

Music competition

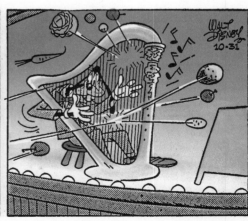

– Later
– A harp?
– Yes! I changed my instrument!

el cine • the cinema

el actor
actor

El héroe se defiende.
The hero fights back.

el proyector
projector

el héroe
hero

la pantalla
screen

la butaca
seat

el pasillo
aisle

Chilla.
He is screaming.

Los espectadores están cautivados.
The viewers are enthralled.

¡ Qué emocionante !
How exciting!

La película da miedo.
The film is scary.

– I just love horror films… I can't see the screen…

– Excuse me, could you take your hat off?

– Arrgh!

el parque • the park

Desliza por el tobogán.
He is sliding down the slide.

la fuente
fountain

el tobogán
slide

el guarda
park attendant

el banco
bench

el columpio
swing

el cochecito
puschair

¡ TENGO SED !

'm thirsty!

los deportes • sport

el estadio • the stadium

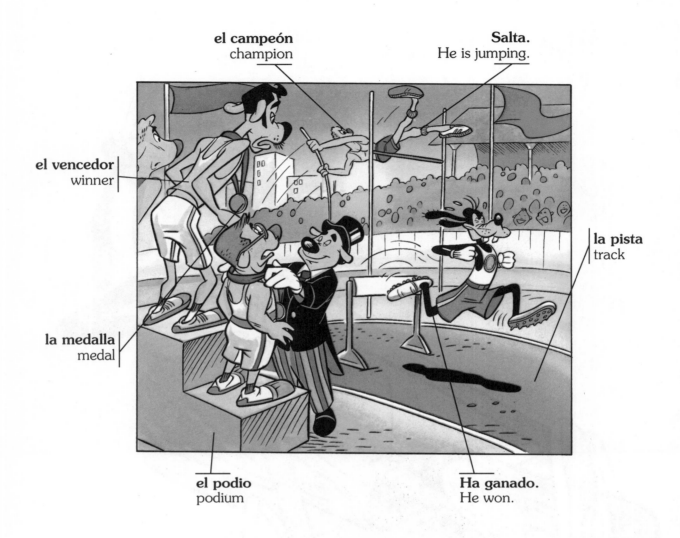

el campeón
champion

Salta.
He is jumping.

el vencedor
winner

la pista
track

la medalla
medal

el podio
podium

Ha ganado.
He won.

Goofy corre.
Goofy is running.

– Forget the other athletes. Concentrate on the race: close your eyes and run!
– You can depend on me!

– Goofy!
– Finish

– I think I can open my eyes now…

el equipo • sportsgear

la red para coger mariposas
butterfly net

el chandal
tracksuit

las pesas
weights

A Morty le gusta jugar al balón.
Morty likes playing ball.

la camiseta
vest

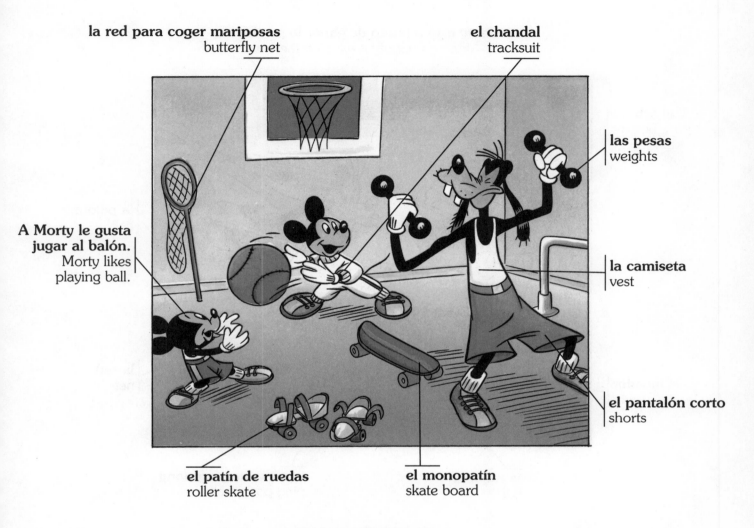

el patín de ruedas
roller skate

el monopatín
skate board

el pantalón corto
shorts

Están en el gimnasio.
They are in the gym.

Minnie prefiere la gimnasia.
Minnie prefers gymnastics.

– I must get a little exercise.

– It really is strong for a butterfly!

– You've given up chasing butterflies?
– Yes, it's too dangerous!

el tenis de mesa • table tennis

Goofy está a punto de ganar la partida.
Goofy is winning the match.

el árbitro umpire

la pelota ball

el jugador player

la red net

la raqueta bat

la mesa de ping pong ping pong table

Es la bola de partido.
It is the match point.

– You play well Goofy, but you wave your arms a lot!
– I'm so excited by the game that I can't keep still.

el esquí • skiing

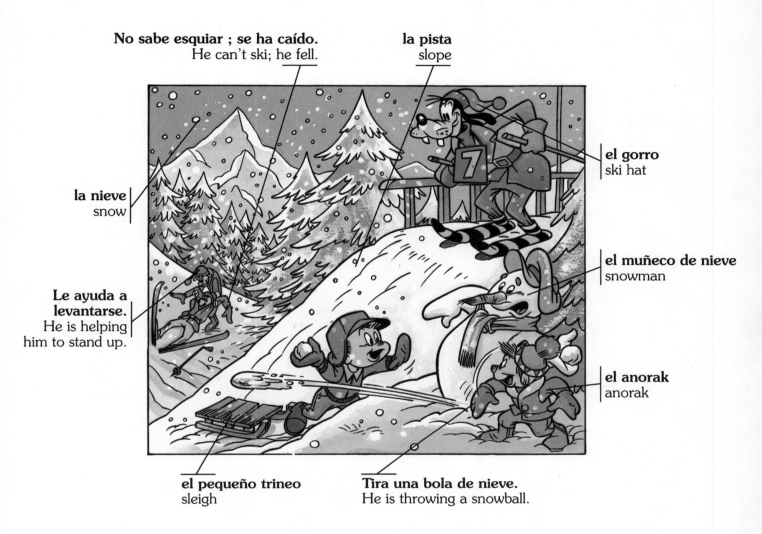

No sabe esquiar ; se ha caído.
He can't ski; he fell.

la pista
slope

el gorro
ski hat

la nieve
snow

el muñeco de nieve
snowman

Le ayuda a levantarse.
He is helping him to stand up.

el anorak
anorak

el pequeño trineo
sleigh

Tira una bola de nieve.
He is throwing a snowball.

Nieva, es el invierno.
It is snowing; it is winter.

Hace frío.
It is cold.

– What a pity you can't be in the race!
– I can't afford skis…

– Starch

– I should have thought of this long ago!

la fiesta • holidays

fiestas navideñas • Christmas

la bola de colores
ball

el Papá Noel
Father Christmas

el árbol de Navidad
Christmas tree

la chimenea
fireplace

la guirnalda
garland

el leño
log

Rirí admira su regalo.
Dewey is admiring his present.

El Papá Noel ha venido.
Father Christmas has come.

– Here's the turkey, Donald!

– Breast or leg?

el picnic • the picnic

el bocadillo
sandwich

la cometa
kite

Jorgito sonríe.
Dewey is smiling.

la hormiga
ant

cámara fotográfica
camera

**Juanito saca
una foto.**
Huey is taking
a photo.

el pollo
chicken

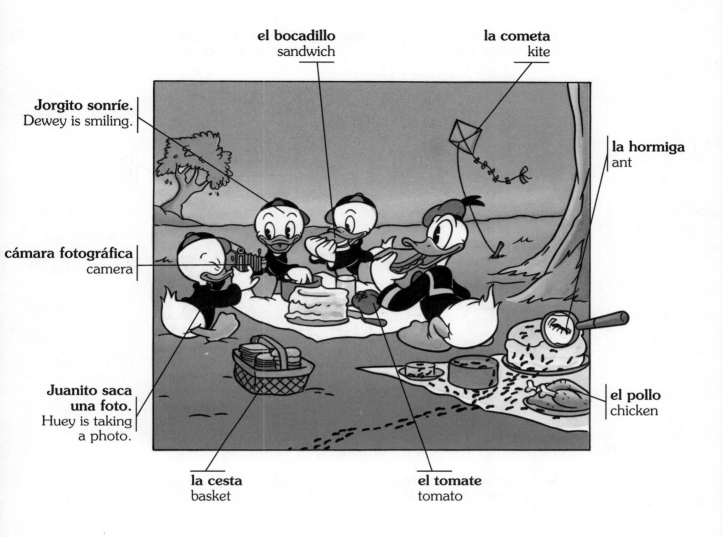

la cesta
basket

el tomate
tomato

Es una comida fría.
It is a cold meal.

Hoy es domingo, todos comen al aire libre ¡ hasta las hormigas !
It is Sunday; everyone is having a picnic, even the ants!

el cumpleaños • the birthday party

Le da un caramelo.
He is giving him a sweet.

Obsequia a Jaimito con un regalo.
He is giving Louie a present.

el zumo de naranja
orange juice

**el pastel
de cumpleaños**
birthday cake

la gaseosa
lemonade

la tableta de chocolate
bar of chocolate

el pirulí
lollipop

Jorgito sopla las velas del pastel.
Huey is blowing out the candles on the cake.

Es el cumpleaños de los sobrinos.
It is the nephews' birthday.

– Our guests haven't come yet…
– … for our birthday party.
– May we eat the ice cream?
– No, wait a little bit longer!

– And now…
– … may we…
– … eat it?
– Okay! You can!

– But first of all, you
should get
changed…

– Invitation.

el circo • the circus

la caballista
rider

el espectador
spectator

la jaula
cage

la pista
ring

el malabarista
juggler

el domador
tamer

el payaso
clown

Es el final del espectáculo.
It is the end of the performance.

Los artistas desfilan.
The performers are parading.

ES UN APARTA-
MENTO MUY BONITO.
ES EL PRIMER PISO
QUE DA AL PATIO.

NO ME
CONVIENE. YO
BUSCO UN
APARTAMENTO
QUE DÉ A
LA CALLE.

TENGO
QUE
DARME
PRISA.

AL SEGUNDO PISO QUE
DA A LA CALLE... VALE
500 DÓLARES
AL MES.

SE
ALQUILA.

¡NO
IMPORTA!
¡QUIERO
VISITARLO!

AQUÍ ESTÁ EL SALÓN...
ADMIRE ESTE CUADRO DEL
SIGLO XIV.

SE
ALQUILA.

t's a beautiful flat, on the first floor
the back.
hat won't do. I'm looking for a flat
at looks onto the street.
or rent

– I have to
hurry!

– Second floor,
overlooking the
street... the rent is
$ 500 per month.
– It doesn't matter!
I'd like to look at it!

– The drawing room... Note this
XIVth century painting...

Annexes

Spanish verbs conjugations

	-ar Verbs	**-er Verbs**	**-ir Verbs**
Infinitive	cant-*ar*	com-*er*	viv-*ir*
Present	canto cantas canta cantamos cantáis cantan	como comes come comemos coméis comen	vivo vives vive vivimos vivís viven
Imperfect	cantaba cantabas cantaba cantábamos cantabais cantaban	comía comías comía comíamos comíais comían	vivía vivías vivía vivíamos vivíais vivían
Simple past	canté cantaste cantó cantemos cantéis canten	comí comiste comió comamos comáis coman	viví viviste vivió vivamos viváis vivan
Future	cantaré cantarás cantará cantaremos cantaréis cantarán	comeré comerás comerá comeremos comeréis comerán	viviré vivirás vivirá viviremos viviréis vivirán
Conditional	cantaría cantarías cantaría cantaríamos cantaríais cantarían	comería comerías comería comeríamos comeríais comerían	viviría vivirías viviría viviríamos viviríais vivirían
Subjunctive present	cante cantes cante cantemos cantéis canten	coma comas coma comamos comáis coman	viva vivas viva vivamos viváis vivan
Subjunctive imperfect	cantara, cantase cantaras, cantases cantara, cantase cantáramos, cantásemos cantarais, cantaseis cantaran, cantasen	comiera, comiese comieras, comieses comiera, comiese comiéramos, comiésemos comierais, comieseis comieran, comiesen	viviera, viviese vivieras, vivieses viviera, viviese viviéramos, viviésemos vivierais, vivieseis vivieran, viviesen
Subjunctive future	cantare cantares cantare cantáremos cantareis cantaren	comiere comieres comiere comiéremos comiereis comieren	viviere vivieres viviere viviéremos viviereis vivieren
Imperative	canta cante cantemos canted canten	come coma comamos comed coman	vive viva vivamos vivid vivan
Present participle	cantando	comiendo	viviendo
Past participle	cantado	comido	vivido

Adjetivos numerales • Numerals

Numerales cardinales • Cardinal numbers

cero	0	nought
uno	1	one
dos	2	two
tres	3	three
cuatro	4	four
cinco	5	five
seis	6	six
siete	7	seven
ocho	8	eight
nueve	9	nine
diez	10	ten

once	11	eleven
doce	12	twelve
trece	13	thirteen
catorce	14	fourteen
quince	15	fifteen
dieciséis	16	sixteen
diecisiete	17	seventeen
dieciocho	18	eighteen
diecinueve	19	nineteen
veinte	20	twenty
veintiuno	21	twenty-one
veintidós	22	twenty-two
treinta	30	thirty
cuarenta	40	forty
cincuenta	50	fifty
sesenta	60	sixty

setenta	70	seventy
setenta y cinco	75	seventy-five
ochenta	80	eighty
ochenta y uno	81	eighty-one
noventa	90	ninety
noventa y uno	91	ninety-one
ciento, cien	100	a/one hundred
ciento uno	101	a hundred and one
ciento dos	102	a hundred and two
ciento cincuenta	150	a hundred and fifty
doscientos	200	two hundred
doscientos uno	201	two hundred and one
doscientos dos	202	two hundred and two
mil	1000	a/one thousand
mil uno	1001	a thousand and one
mil dos	1002	a thousand and two
dos mil	2000	two thousand
un millón	1000000	a/one million
dos millones	2000000	two million

Numerales ordinales
Ordinal numbers

primero	1°	1st	first
segundo	2°	2nd	second
tercero	3°	3rd	third
cuarto	4°	4th	fourth
quinto	5°	5th	fifth
sexto	6°	6th	sixth
séptimo	7°	7th	seventh
octavo	8°	8th	eighth
noveno	9°	9th	ninth
décimo	10°	10th	tenth
undécimo, onceno	11°	11th	eleventh
duodécimo	12°	12th	twelfth
decimotercero	13°	13th	thirteenth
decimocuarto	14°	14th	fourteenth
decimoquinto	15°	15th	fifteenth
decimosexto	16°	16th	sixteenth
decimoséptimo	17°	17th	seventeenth
decimoctavo	18°	18th	eighteenth
decimonono	19°	19th	nineteenth
vigésimo	20°	20th	twentieth
vigésimo primero	21°	21st	twenty-first
vigésimo segundo	22°	22nd	twenty-second
trigésimo	30°	30th	thirtieth

¿ Qué hora es ?
What time is it?

4.00 **Son las cuatro.**
It is four o'clock.

4.05 **Son las cuatro y cinco.**
It is five (minutes) past four.

4.15 **Son las cuatro y cuarto.**
It is (a) quarter past four.

4.30 **Son las cuatro y media.**
It is half past four. / It is four thirty.

4.45 **Son las cinco menos cuarto.**
It is (a) quarter to five.

4.50 **Son las cinco menos diez.**
It is ten to five.

Son las doce. / Es mediodía.
It is twelve o'clock. / It is noon.

Son las doce. / Es medianoche.
It is twelve o'clock. / It is midnight.

la fecha • the date

los días days		**los meses** months	
lunes	Monday	**enero**	January
martes	Tuesday	**febrero**	February
miércoles	Wednesday	**marzo**	March
jueves	Thursday	**abril**	April
viernes	Friday	**mayo**	May
sábado	Saturday	**junio**	June
domingo	Sunday	**julio**	July
		agosto	August
		septiembre	September
		octubre	October
		noviembre	November
		diciembre	December

Jueves, 1° de mayo de 1994
(mil novecientos noventa y cuatro)
Thursday, 1st May 1994

Viernes, 2 de mayo de 1994
(mil novecientos noventa y cuatro)
Friday, 2nd May 1994

Sábado, 3 de mayo de 1994
(mil novecientos noventa y cuatro)
Saturday, 3rd May 1994

Domingo, 4 de mayo de 1994
(mil novecientos noventa y cuatro)
Sunday, 4th May 1994

Table of phonetic symbols

Pronunciation of Spanish

Vowels

[i] idea, nariz
[e] cabeza, negocio

[a] bajo, calle
[o] pequeño, personaje

Semi-consonants

[j] labio, silencio
[ĭ] sequía, ley

[w] cuadro, persuadir
[ŭ] europeo, gaucho

Consonants

[p] perro, golpe
[b] batalla, vaca
[β] levantarse, dibujo
[t] sentar
[d] debajo, duro
[ð] ensalada, necesidad
[k] cabeza, queso, kilómetro
[g] gato, gordo
[ɣ] delgado, hormiga
[f] difícil, fuego
[s] saber, poseer
[z] mismo
[tʃ] chocolate, estrecho
[θ] despacio, nariz
[l] librería, delante
[ʎ] estrella, llamar
[r] amar, porque
[r̄] derrota, rojo
[m] momento
[ɱ] influencia, inferior
[n] negro, enorme
[ŋ] inglés, ingenuo
[ɲ] mañana, niño
[x] hoja, gente
['] *primary stress mark
precedes a syllable*

Index

Abbreviations

adj	adjective
adv.	adverb
f.	feminine
interj.	interjection
inv.	invariable
m.	masculine
n.	noun
pl.	plural
v.	verb

Spanish – English

A

abeja [aˈβexa] *n. f.* : bee **63**
abeto [aˈβeto] *n. m.* : fir tree **64**
abierto, ta [aˈβjerto, ta] *adj.* : open **30**
abono [aˈβono] *n. m.* : fertilizer **52**
abrigo [aˈβriɣo] *n. m.* : coat **40**
abrir * [aˈβrir] *v.* : open **84**
abuela [aˈβwela] *n. f.* : grandmother **34**
abuelo [aˈβwelo] *n. m.* : grandfather **34**
acera [aˈθera] *n. f.* : pavement **18**
actor, triz [aɣˈtor, ˈtriθ] *n.* : actor, tress **80**
acuario [aˈkwarjo] *n. m.* : fish bowl **11**
admirar [aðmiˈrar] *v.* : admire **90**
aduana [aˈðwana] *n. f.* : customs *n. pl.* **72**
aduanero, ra [aðwaˈnero, ra] *n.* : customs officer **72**
aeropuerto [aeroˈpwerto] *n. m.* : airport **72**
agitado, da [axiˈtaðo, ða] *adj.* : hectic **66**
agua [ˈaɣwa] *n. f.* : water **57**
águila [ˈaɣila] *n. f.* : eagle **60, 61**
aguja [aˈɣuxa] *n. f.* : hand **31**
ahora [aˈora] *adv.* : now **66, 72, 92**
ajedrez [axeˈðreθ] *n. m.* : chess **75**
ala [ˈala] *n. f.* : breast **90**
alameda [alaˈmeða] *n. f.* : path **8**
albornoz [alβorˈnoθ] *n. m.* : bathrobe **15**
alegre [aˈleɣre] *adj.* : happy **15**
alfombra [alˈfombra] *n. f.* : rug **12**
almidón [almiˈðon] *n. m.* : starch **87**
almohada [almoˈaða] *n. f.* : pillow **13**
almuerzo [almˈwerθo] *n. m.* : lunch **56**
alquilar [alkiˈlar] *v.* : rent **9, 93**
alto, ta [ˈalto, ta] *adj.* : tall **36**
alumno, na [aˈlumno, na] *n.* : pupil **26**
amable [aˈmaβle] *adj.* : nice **38**
amarillo, lla [amaˈriʎo, ʎa] *adj.* : yellow **29**
ambulancia [ambuˈlanθja] *n. f.* : ambulance **49**
americana [ameriˈkana] *n. f.* : jacket **40**
amigo, ga [aˈmiɣo, ɣa] *n.* : friend **27**
ancla [ˈaŋkla] *n. f.* : anchor **65**
ancho, cha [ˈantʃo, tʃa] *adj.* : big **40**
andén [anˈden] *n. m.* : platform **22**
anillo [aˈniʎo] *n. m.* : ring **43**
animal [aniˈmal] *n. m.* : animal **68, 69, 76**
anorak [anoˈrak] *n. m.* : anorak **87**
aparcamiento [aparkaˈmjento] *n. m.* : car park **18**
aparcar [aparˈkar] *v.* : park **18**
apariencias [apaˈrjenθjas] *n. f. pl.* : appearances *n. pl.* **27**
apartamento [apartaˈmento] *n. m.* : flat **93**
aplaudir [aplauˈðir] *v.* : clap **78**
apostarse * [aposˈtarse] *v.* : bet * **52**
aprender [aprenˈder] *v.* : learn * **27, 30**
árbitro, tra [ˈarβitro, tra] *n.* : umpire **86**
árbol [ˈarβol] *n. m.* : tree **8, 60, 90**
ardilla [arˈðiʎa] *n. f.* : squirrel **60**
arena [aˈrena] *n. f.* : sand **73**
armario [arˈmarjo] *n. m.* : wardrobe **12**
armario empotrado [arˈmarjoempoˈtraðo] *m.* : cupboard **14**
arpa [ˈarpa] *n. f.* : harp **79**
arroyo [aˈrōjo] *n. m.* : brook **62**
arroz [aˈroθ] *n. m.* : rice **56**

artista [arˈtista] *n.* : artist **77**; performer **93**
asar [aˈsar] *v.* : grill **74**
aspecto físico [asˈpeɣtoˈfisiko] *m.* : appearance **36**
atasco [aˈtasko] *n. m.* : traffic jam **18, 19**
aterrizar * [ateˈrīˈθar] *v.* : land **72**
atleta [aˈðleta] *n.* : athlete **84**
aula [ˈaula] *n. f.* : classroom **26**
aumento [auˈmento] *n. m.* : raise **28**
autobús [autoˈβus] *n. m.* : bus **23**
autocar de camping [autoˈkardeˈkampiɲ] *m.* : camping car **74**
avestruz [aβesˈtruθ] *n. m.* : ostrich **76**
avión [aˈβjon] *n. m.* : (aero)plane **66, 72**
ayuda [aˈjuða] *n. f.* : help **26**
ayudar [ajuˈðar] *v.* : help **28, 87**
azafata [aθaˈfata] *n. f.* : air hostess **72**
azúcar [aˈθukar] *n. m.* : sugar **21, 55**
azucarero [aθukaˈrero] *n. m.* : sugar dispenser **55**
azul [aˈθul] *adj.* : blue **29**

B

bailar [baiˈlar] *v.* : dance **79**
baile [ˈbaile] *n. m.* : dance **39**
bajo, ja [ˈbaxo, xa] *adj.* : small **36**
balcón [balˈkon] *n. m.* : balcony **9**
balón [baˈlon] *n. m.* : ball **85**
banco [ˈbaŋko] *n. m.* : bench **81**
bañera [baˈɲera] *n. f.* : bath **15**
tomar un baño [toˈmarunˈbaɲo] : have * a bath **15**
barandilla [baranˈdiʎa] *n. f.* : bannisters *n. pl.* **10**
barato, ta [baˈrato, ta] *adj.* : cheap **21**
barba [ˈbarβa] *n. f.* : beard **37**
barbilla [barˈβiʎa] *n. f.* : chin **48**
barco [ˈbarko] *n. m.* : boat **65**
barómetro [baˈrometro] *n. m.* : barometer **67**
bata [ˈbata] *n. f.* : dressing gown **13**
batería [bateˈria] *n. f.* : drums *n. pl.* **79**
beber [beˈβer] *v.* : drink * **55**
bici [ˈbiθi] *n. f.* : bike **19**
bicicleta [biθiˈkleta] *n. f.* : bicycle **18**
bien [bjen] *adv.* : well **34, 77, 86**
bien educado, da [bjeneduˈkaðo, ða] : polite **38**
bigote [biˈɣote] *n. m.* : moustache **37**
billete [biˈʎete] *n. m.* : bank note **21**
billete de autobús [biˈʎetedeautoˈβus] *m.* : bus fare **28**
blanco, ca [ˈblaŋko, ka] *adj.* : white **29**
blusa [ˈblusa] *n. f.* : blouse **39**
boca [ˈboka] *n. f.* : mouth **48**
bocadillo [bokaˈðiʎo] *n. m.* : sandwich **91**
bola [ˈbola] *n. f.* : ball **90**
bola de nieve [ˈboladeˈnjeβe] *f.* : snowball **87**
bolígrafo [boˈliɣrafo] *n. m.* : pen **28**
bonito, ta [boˈnito, ta] *adj.* : lovely **9, 31, 39**; beautiful **93**
bosque [ˈboske] *n. m.* : forest **60**
bostezar * [bosteˈθar] *v.* : yawn **13**
bota [ˈbota] *n. f.* : boot **42**
botella [boˈteʎa] *n. f.* : bottle **56**
botín [boˈtin] *n. m.* : ankle boot **42**
boya [ˈboja] *n. f.* : rubber ring **73**
brazo [ˈbraθo] *n. m.* : arm **35, 47**

brillar [briˈʎar] *v.* : shine * **66**; glitter **43**
broche [ˈbrotʃe] *n. m.* : brooch **43**
bueno, buen, buena [ˈbweno, bwen, ˈbwena] *adj.* : good **29, 79**
buque [ˈbuke] *n. m.* : ship **65**
buscar [busˈkar] *v.* : look for **93**
ir* a buscar [irabusˈkar] : pick up **37**
butaca [buˈtaka] *n. f.* : seat **80**

C

caballista [kaβaˈʎista] *n. m.* : rider **93**
caballo [kaˈβaʎo] *n. m.* : horse **68**
cabellos [kaˈβeʎos] *n. m. pl.* : hair **37**
cabeza [kaˈβeθa] *n. f.* : head **46**
cabina telefónica [kaˈβinateleˈfonika] *f.* : telephone kiosk **19**
cabra [ˈkaβra] *n. f.* : goat **62**
caer * [kaˈer] *v.* : fall * **60**
caerse * [kaˈerse] *v.* : fall * **87**
café [kaˈfe] *n. m.* : coffee **55**
cafetera [kafeˈtera] *n. f.* : coffee-pot **55**
caja [ˈkaxa] *n. f.* : cash register **21**
cajero, ra [kaˈxero, ra] *n.* : cashier **21**
cajón [kaˈxon] *n. m.* : drawer **41**
calabaza [kalaˈbaθa] *n. f.* : pumpkin **52**
calcetín [kalθeˈtin] *n. m.* : sock **41**
cálculo [ˈkalkulo] *n. m.* : arithmetic **28**
calentarse [kalenˈtarse] *v.* : warm oneself **74**
calzado [kalˈθaðo] *n. m.* : shoes *n. pl.* **42**
callarse [kaˈʎarse] *v.* : keep * one's mouth shut **3**
calle [ˈkaʎe] *n. f.* : street **18, 93**
cama [ˈkama] *n. f.* : bed **13**
cámara fotográfica [ˈkamarafotoˈɣrafika] *f.* : camera **91**
cambiar [kamˈbjar] *v.* : change **79**
cambiarse de ropa [kamˈbjarsedeˈropa] : get changed **92**
camello [kaˈmeʎo] *n. m.* : camel **76**
camino [kaˈmino] *n. m.* : track **61**
camión [kaˈmjon] *n. m.* : lorry **23**
camisa [kaˈmisa] *n. f.* : shirt **41**
camiseta [kamiˈseta] *n. f.* : tee-shirt **41**; vest **8**
campeón, na [kampeˈon, na] *n.* : champion **8**
camping [ˈkampiɲ] *n. m.* : camping **74**
ir* de camping [irdeˈkampiɲ] : camp **74**
campo [ˈkampo] *n. m.* : country(side) **62**
canguro [kaŋˈguro] *n. m.* : kangaroo **76**
"canguro" [kaŋˈguro] *n.* : babysitter **37**
canica [kaˈnika] *n. f.* : marble **27**
canoa [kaˈnoa] *n. f.* : canoe **64**
cansado, da [kanˈsaðo, ða] *adj.* : tired **13**
cantante [kanˈtante] *n.* : singer **79**
caña de pescar [ˈkaɲadepesˈkar] *f.* : fishing rod **64**
cara [ˈkara] *n. f.* : face **48**
caramelo [karaˈmelo] *n. m.* : sweet **28, 92**
caravana [karaˈβana] *n. f.* : caravan **74**
carne [ˈkarne] *n. f.* : meat **56, 74**
carnicería [karniθeˈria] *n. f.* : butcher's shop **2**
carnicero, ra [karniˈθero, ra] *n.* : butcher **20**
caro, ra [ˈkaro, ra] *adj.* : expensive **21, 77**
carrera [kaˈrera] *n. f.* : race **84**

rtera [kar'tera] *n. f.* : wallet **21**; satchel **28**
rtero [kar'tero] *n. m.* : postman **18**
sa ['kasa] *n. f.* : house **7, 9, 10, 67, 68**
silla [ka'siʎa] *n. f.* : kennel **68**
staña [kas'taɲa] *n. f.* : chestnut **60**
stillo de arena [kas'tiʎodea'rena] *m.* : sand castle **73**
utivar [kaŭti'βar] *v.* : enthrall **80**
zar [ka'θar] *v.* : hunt **38**
zuela [ka'θwela] *n. f.* : saucepan **14**
bolla [θe'βoʎa] *n. f.* : onion **52**
bra ['θeβra] *n. f.* : zebra **69, 76**
ja ['θexa] *n. f.* : eyelash **48**
na ['θena] *n. f.* : dinner **57**
pillarse los dientes [θepi'ʎarselos'djentes] : brush one's teeth **15**
pillo de dientes [θe'piʎode'djentes] *m.* : toothbrush **15**
rcado [θer'kaðo] *n. m.* : fence **62**
rdo ['θerðo] *n. m.* : pig **62, 68**
reales [θere'ales] *n. m. pl.* : cereal **55**
reza [θe'reθa] *n. f.* : cherry **53**
rrado, da [θe'ɾaðo, ða] *adj.* : closed **9, 20, 30**
rradura [θeɾa'dura] *n. f.* : lock **9**
rrar [θe'ɾar] *v.* : close* **84**
sped ['θespeð] *n. m.* : lawn **8**
sta ['θesta] *n. f.* : basket **91**
lo ['θjelo] *n. m.* : sky **66**
rvo ['θjerβo] *n. m.* : stag **76**
ra ['θifra] *n. f.* : figure **28**
ae ['θine] *n. m.* : cinema **80**
turón [θintu'ron] *n. m.* : belt **41**
co ['θirko] *n. m.* : circus **93**
culo ['θirkulo] *n. m.* : circle **30**
dad [θju'ðað] *n. f.* : town **17, 29**
aro, ra ['klaro, ra] *adj.* : light **29**
aro del bosque ['klarodel'boske] *m.* : clearing **60**
ase ['klase] *n. f.* : class **26**
vel [kla'βel] *n. m.* : carnation **63**
che ['kotʃe] *n. m.* : car **18, 19**
checito [kotʃe'θito] *n. m.* : puschair **81**
cina [ko'θina] *n. f.* : kitchen **14, 57**; cooker **14**
cinar [koθi'nar] *v.* : cook **14**
codrilo [koko'ðrilo] *n. m.* : crocodile **69**
do ['koðo] *n. m.* : elbow **47**
ger [ko'xer] *v.* : catch* **76**
l [kol] *n. f.* : cabbage **52**
la de caballo ['koladeka'βaʎo] *f.* : ponytail **37**
chón [kol'tʃon] *n. m.* : mattress **12**
gar [kol'ɣar] *v.* : hang* up **67**
lor [ko'lor] *n. m.* : colour **29**
lumpio [ko'lumpjo] *n. m.* : swing **81**
llar [ko'ʎar] *n. m.* : necklace **43**
mer [ko'mer] *v.* : eat* **54, 56, 60, 77, 92**
meta [ko'meta] *n. f.* : kite **66, 91**
mida [ko'miða] *n. f.* : food **51**; meal **91**
modo, da ['komoðo, da] *adj.* : comfortable **11**
mprar [kom'prar] *v.* : buy* **9, 21, 52**
de compras ['irde'kompras] : shop **20**
mprobar* [kompro'βar] *v.* : check **20**
ncentrarse [konθen'trarse] *v.* : concentrate **84**
ncierto [kon'θjerto] *n. m.* : concert **78, 79**
ncurso [koŋ'kurso] *n. m.* : competition **79**
ncha ['kontʃa] *n. f.* : shell **73**
nducir* [kondu'θir] *v.* : drive* **23, 62**
nductor, ra [konduɣ'tor, ra] *n.* : driver **23**
nejo [ko'nexo] *n. m.* : rabbit **62**
nstruir [konstrw'ir] *v.* : build* **64**
ntento, ta [kon'tento, ta] *adj.* : happy **30, 31, 38**; glad **74**
ntraventana [kontraben'tana] *n. f.* : shutter **9**
nvidado, da [kombi'ðaðo, ða] *n.* : guest **92**
razón [kora'θon] *n. m.* : heart **49**
rbata [kor'βata] *n. f.* : tie **39**
rbata de pajarita [kor'βatadepaxa'rita] *f.* : bow tie **39**
rdón [kor'ðon] *n. m.* : shoelace **42**
rreos [ko'ɾeos] *n. m. pl.* : post office **18**
rrer [ko'ɾer] *v.* : run* **27, 69, 84**
rtacésped [korta'θespeð] *n. m.* : lawn mower **8**

cortar [kor'tar] *v.* : cut* **35**
corto, ta ['korto, ta] *adj.* : short **37, 40**
corzo ['korθo] *n. m.* : deer *n. inv.* **61**
crecer* [kre'θer] *v.* : grow* **52**
creer* [kre'er] *v.* : believe **9**; think* **35, 43**
cruce ['kruθe] *n. m.* : crossroads *n. pl.* **18**
cruzar* (la calle) [kru'θar(la'kaʎe)] *v.* : cross (the street) **18, 19**
cuaderno [kwa'ðerno] *n. m.* : exercise book **28**
cuadrado [kwa'ðraðo] *n. m.* : square **30**
cuadro ['kwaðro] *n. m.* : painting **77, 93**
cuarto de baño ['kwartode'baɲo] *m.* : bathroom **15**
cuarto de estar ['kwartodees'tar] *m.* : sitting-room **11**
cubo ['kuβo] *n. m.* : building block **75**
cubo de la basura ['kuβodelaba'sura] *m.* : dustbin **14**
cuchara [ku'tʃara] *n. f.* : spoon **54**
cucharón [kutʃa'ron] *n. m.* : ladle **57**
cuchillo [ku'tʃiʎo] *n. m.* : knife **54**
cuello ['kweʎo] *n. m.* : neck **46, 69**
cuerpo ['kwerpo] *n. m.* : body **46, 47**
cuidar [kwi'ðar] *v.* : look after **49**
cumbre ['kumbre] *n. f.* : peak **61**
cumpleaños [kumple'aɲos] *n. m. inv.* : birthday **92**

CH

chalet [tʃa'let] *n. m.* : chalet **61**
champú [tʃam'pu] *n. m.* : shampoo **15**
chandal [tʃan'dal] *n. m.* : tracksuit **85**
chaqueta [tʃa'keta] *n. f.* : jacket **39**
charca ['tʃarka] *n. f.* : pond **68**
charco ['tʃarko] *n. m.* : puddle **67**
chica ['tʃika] *n. f.* : girl **39**
chillar [tʃi'ʎar] *v.* : scream **80**
chimenea [tʃime'nea] *n. f.* : fireplace **90**; chimney **9**
chocolate [tʃoko'late] *n. m.* : chocolate **92**

D

dar* [dar] *v.* : give* **92**
darse* prisa ['darse'prisa] : hurry **93**
¡ de acuerdo ! [dea'kwerðo] *interj.* : okay ! **92**
deberes [de'βeres] *n. m. pl.* : homework **28**
decidir [deθi'ðir] *v.* : decide **68**
decir* [de'θir] *v.* : say* **42**; tell* **52**
dedo ['deðo] *n. m.* : finger **47**
dedo del pie ['deðodel'pje] *m.* : toe **47**
dejar [de'xar] *v.* : let* **13**; leave* **54**
delantal [delan'tal] *n. m.* : smock **77**
delgado, da [del'ɣaðo, ða] *adj.* : thin **36**
defenderse [defen'derse] *v.* : fight* back **80**
delicioso, sa [deli'θjoso, sa] *adj.* : delicious **56, 60**
demasiado [dema'sjaðo] *adv.* : too **40, 42, 62, 85**
dentífrico [den'tifriko] *n. m.* : toothpaste **15**
estar* de pie [es'tarde'pje] : be* standing up **47**
deporte [de'porte] *n. m.* : sport **83**
deprisa [de'prisa] *adv.* : quickly **69**
desafinar [desafi'nar] *v.* : sing* out of tune **79**
desayuno [desa'juno] *n. m.* : breakfast **55**
desfilar [desfi'lar] *v.* : parade **93**
deslizar [dezli'θar] *v.* : slide* **81**
desorden [de'sorðen] *n. m.* : mess **34**
despacho [des'patʃo] *n. m.* : desk **26**
despegar* [despe'ɣar] *v.* : take* off **72**
despertador [desperta'ðor] *n. m.* : alarm-clock **12, 31**
despertarse [desper'tarse] *v.* : wake* up **12**
día ['dia] *n. m.* : day **68**
diente ['djente] *n. m.* : tooth **15, 48**
dinamita [dina'mita] *n. f.* : dynamite **19**
dinero [di'nero] *n. m.* : money **21**
diploma [di'ploma] *n. m.* : diploma **47**
dirección [direɣ'θjon] *n. f.* : direction **23**

director, ra [direɣ'tor, ra] *n.* : headmaster *n. m.* **26**
director de orquesta [direk'tordeor'kesta] *m.* : conductor **78**
disco ['disko] *n. m.* : record **37**
divertirse* [diβer'tirse] *v.* : have* fun **27, 42, 75**
división [diβi'sjon] *n. f.* : division **28**
dólar ['dolar] *n. m.* : dollar **28, 47**
dolerle* a uno la cabeza [do'lerlea'unolaka'βeθa] : have* a headache **49**
domador, ra [doma'ðor, ra] *n.* : tamer **93**
dominó [domi'no] *n. m.* : domino **75**
dormir* [dor'mir] *v.* : sleep* **13, 74**
dormirse* [dor'mirse] *v.* : fall* asleep **62**

E

edificio [eði'fiθjo] *n. m.* : building **18**
edredón [eðre'ðon] *n. m.* : eiderdown **13**
eléctrico, ca [e'leɣtriko, ka] *adj.* : electric **79**
elefante [ele'fante] *n. m.* : elephant **69**
elegante [ele'ɣante] *adj.* : smart **39**
empapelar [empape'lar] *v.* : paper **69**
enaguas [e'naɣwas] *n. f. pl.* : petticoat **39**
encontrar* [eŋkon'trar] *v.* : find* **39, 60, 61**
enfermera [eɱfer'mera] *n. f.* : nurse **49**
enfermo, ma [eɱ'fermo, ma] *adj.* : sick **49**
entender* [enten'der] *v.* : understand* **30**
equipaje [eki'paxe] *n. m.* : luggage **22**
equipo [ekipo] *n. m.* : sportsgear **85**
equipo estereofónico [e'kipoestereo'foniko] *m.* : stereo **11**
equivocarse [ekiβo'karse] *v.* : make* a mistake **28**
escalera [eska'lera] *n. f.* : stairs *n. pl.* **10**
escalón [eska'lon] *n. m.* : step **10**
escarpín [eskar'pin] *n. m.* : court shoe **42**
escena [es'θena] *n. f.* : stage **78**
escoger* [esko'xer] *v.* : choose* **69**
escollera [esko'ʎera] *n. f.* : jetty **65**
esconderse [eskon'derse] *v.* : hide* **76**
escribir* [eskri'βir] *v.* : write*
escuchar [eskut'ʃar] *v.* : listen **30**
escuela [es'kwela] *n. f.* : school **25, 26, 27, 30**
esmeralda [esme'ralda] *n. f.* : emerald **43**
espalda [es'palda] *n. f.* : back **46**
espectáculo [espeɣ'takulo] *n. m.* : performance **93**
espectador, ra [espeɣta'ðor, ra] *n.* : spectator **93**; viewer **80**
espejo [es'pexo] *n. m.* : mirror **15**
esperar [espe'rar] *v.* : wait (for) **23, 60, 62, 69, 92**; hope **29**
esponja [es'poɲxa] *n. f.* : sponge **14**
esquí [es'ki] *n. m.* : ski **87**; skiing **87**
esquiar [eski'ar] *v.* : ski **87**
hacer* esquí náutico [a'θeres'ki'naŭtiko] : water-ski* **65**
estación [esta'θjon] *n. f.* : station **22**
estadio [es'taðjo] *n. m.* : stadium **84**
estantería [estante'ria] *n. f.* : shelf **14**
estar* [es'tar] *v.* : be* **21, 85**
estar* en el paro [es'tarenel'paro] : be* out of work **36**
estrecho, cha [es'tretʃo, tʃa] *adj.* : narrow **10**
estrella [es'treʎa] *n. f.* : star **66**
excelente [esθe'lente] *adj.* : excellent **26**
explicación [esplika'θjon] *n. f.* : explanation **65**
explicar* [espli'kar] *v.* : explain **63**
exprimidor [esprimi'ðor] *n. m.* : orange squeezer **36**
extraño, ña [es'traɲo, ɲa] *adj.* : strange **42**

F

falda ['falda] *n. f.* : skirt **40**
familia [fa'milja] *n. f.* : family **34**
famoso, sa [fa'moso, sa] *adj.* : famous **38**

faro ['faro] n. m. : headlight **19**; lighthouse **65**
feliz [fe'liθ] adj. : happy **35**
feo, fea ['feo, 'fea] adj. : ugly **36**
fiel [fjel] adj. : faithful **68**
fiesta ['fjesta] n. f. : holiday **89**
final [fi'nal] n. m. : end **93**
flauta ['flaŭta] n. f. : flute **78**
flequillo [fle'kiʎo] n. m. : fringe **37**
flor [flor] n. f. : flower **8, 63**
florero [flo'rero] n. m. : vase **11**
florista [flo'rista] n. : florist **63**
fluir *[flwir] v. : flow **64**
forma ['forma] n. f. : shape **30**
foto ['foto] n. f. : photo **46, 91**
sacar una foto [sa'karuna'foto] : take* a photo **46, 91**
fregadero [freɣa'ðero] n. m. : sink **14**
fregar los platos [fre'ɣarlos'platos] : do* the dishes **14**
frente ['frente] n. f. : forehead **48**
fresa ['fresa] n. f. : strawberry **53**
frío, fría ['frio, 'fria] adj. : cold **74, 87, 91**
fruncir el ceño [frun'θirel'θeɲo] : frown **46**
fruta ['fruta] n. f. : fruit **53**
fuego ['fweɣo] n. m. : fire **74**
fuente ['fwente] n. f. : fountain **81**; dish **54**
fuerte ['fwerte] adj. : strong **36, 85**
furioso, sa [fur'joso, sa] adj. : angry **57**

G

gafas ['gafas] n. f. pl. : glasses n. pl. **46**
gafas de sol ['gafasde'sol] f. pl. : sunglasses n. pl. **73**
gallina [ga'ʎina] n. f. : hen **68**
gallinero [gaʎi'nero] n. m. : henhouse **68**
gallo ['gaʎo] n. m. : cock **68**
gamuza [ga'muθa] n. f. : chamois **61**
ganar [ga'nar] v. : win* **84, 86**
garaje [ga'raxe] n. m. : garage **9**
gaseosa [gase'osa] n. f. : lemonade **92**
gato, ta ['gato, ta] n. : cat **68**
gaviota [ga'βjota] n. f. : seagull **66**
gente ['xente] n. f. : people **33**
gimnasia [xim'nasia] n. f. : gymnastics n. pl. **85**
gimnasio [xim'nasjo] n. m. : gym **85**
goma ['goma] n. f. : rubber **77**
gordo, da ['gorðo, ða] adj. : fat **36**
gorra ['goṝa] n. f. : cap **40**
gorro ['goṝo] n. m. : cap **41**; ski hat **87**
gorro de dormir ['goṝodedor'mir] m. : nightcap **13**
¡ gracias ! ['graθjas] interj. : thanks ! **28, 36**
grande ['grande] adj. : big **42**
granja ['granxa] n. f. : farm **68**
granjero, ra [gran'xero, ra] n. : farmer **68**
grifo ['grifo] n. m. : tap **15**
gris [gris] adj. : grey **29**
guardarropa [gwarða'ṝopa] n. m. : wardrobe **41**
guijarro [gi'xaṝo] n. m. : pebble **64**
guirnalda [gir'nalda] n. f. : garland **90**
guisante [gi'sante] n. m. : pea **52**
guitarra [gi'taṝa] n. f. : guitar **74, 79**
gustarle a uno [gus'tarlea'uno] v. : like **57**

H

habitación [aβita'θjon] n. f. : bedroom **12**
hablar [a'βlar] v. : talk* **76**
hacer* la limpieza [ha'θerlalim'pjeθa] : clean up **34**
tener* hambre [te'ner'ambre] : be* hungry **54**
hambriento, ta [am'brjento, ta] adj. : starving **77**
hangar [aŋ'gar] n. m. : hangar **72**
¡ hasta la vista ! ['astala'βista] interj. : bye ! **8**
¡ hasta luego ! ['asta'lweɣo] interj. : bye ! **14**
¡ hasta pronto ! ['asta'pronto] interj. : see you soon ! **8, 22**

helado [e'laðo] n. m. : ice cream **92**
hermoso, sa [er'moso, sa] adj. : beautiful **62**; lovely **53**
héroe ['eroe] n. m. : hero **80**
hierba ['j(dʒ)erβa] n. f. : grass **60**
hijo, hija ['ixo, 'ixa] n. : son **34**, daughter **34**; child **35**
hipopótamo [ipo'potamo] n. m. : hippopotamus **69**
hoja ['oxa] n. f. : leaf **60**
hombre ['ombre] n. m. : man **35**
hombro ['ombro] n. m. : shoulder **46**
hora ['ora] n. f. : hour **31, 35**; time **14, 31**
hormiga [or'miɣa] n. f. : ant **91**
horno ['orno] n. m. : oven **14**
hortalizas [orta'liθas] n. f. pl. : vegetables n. pl. **52**
hospital [ospi'tal] n. m. : hospital **49**
hoy [oĭ] adv. : today **27, 60, 72**
huella ['weʎa] n. f. : track **30**
hueso ['(g)weso] n. m. : bone **54**
huevo ['(g)weβo] n. m. : egg **55, 60, 61**
humano, na [u'mano, na] adj. : human **45**
humo ['umo] n. m. : smoke **74**
hundirse [un'dirse] v. : sink* **64**

I

idea [i'ðea] n. f. : idea **66, 68**
impermeable [imperme'aβle] n. m. : raincoat **40, 67**
imposible [impo'siβle] adj. : impossible **9**
indicar* el camino [indi'karelka'mino] : show* the way **18**
Indio, ia ['indjo, ja] n. : Indian **64**
indio, ia ['indjo, ja] adj. : Indian **38**
influencia [imflw'enθja] n. f. : influence **26**
instrumento [instru'mento] n. m. : instrument **79**
intentar [inten'tar] v. : try* **65**
invierno [im'bjerno] n. m. : winter **87**
invitación [imbita'θjon] n. f. : invitation **92**
invitado, da [inbi'taðo, ða] n. : guest **40**
invitar [imbi'tar] v. : invite **38**
inyección [indʒeɣ'θjon] n. f. : injection **49**
ir *[ir] v. : go* **20, 39, 57, 76**
irse* a acostar ['irseaakos'tar] : go* to bed **75**

J

jabón [xa'βon] n. m. : soap **15**
jardín [xaʀ'ðin] n. m. : garden **8, 69**
jaula ['xaŭla] n. f. : cage **93**
jefe ['xefe] n. m. : chief **38**
jeringuilla [xeriɲ'giʎa] n. f. : syringe **49**
jersey [xer'seĭ] n. m. : pullover **41**
jirafa [xi'rafa] n. f. : giraffe **69, 76**
joven ['xoβen] adj. : young **35**
joyas ['xojas] n. f. pl. : jewellery **43**
judía verde [xu'ðia'berðe] f. : green bean **52**
juego ['xweɣo] n. m. : game **75**
juego de damas ['xweɣode'damas] m. : checkers n. pl. **75**
jugador, ora [xuɣa'ðor, ora n. : player **86**
jugar *[xu'ɣar] v. : play **27, 75, 85, 86**
juguete [xu'ɣete] n. m. : toy **75**

K

kilo ['kilo] n. m. : kilo **20**

L

lacio, ia ['laθjo, ja] adj. : straight **37**
lámpara ['lampara] n. f. : lamp **12**

lápiz ['lapiθ] n. m. : pencil **77**
largo, ga ['larɣo, ɣa] adj. : long **37, 69**
lavabo [la'βaβo] n. m. : hand basin **15**
lavarse [la'βarse] v. : wash oneself **15**
leche ['letʃe] n. f. : milk **21, 55**
lechuga [le'tʃuɣa] n. f. : lettuce **52**
lechuza [le'tʃuθa] n. f. : owl **66**
leer *[le'er] v. : read* **11**
lengua ['lengwa] n. f. : tongue **48**
leña ['leɲa] n. f. : wood **74**
leño ['leɲo] n. m. : log **90**
león, na [le'on, na] n. : lion **69**
levantarse [leβan'tarse] v. : get* up **12**
libro ['liβro] n. m. : book **11, 27, 30**
hacer* la limpieza [ha'θerlalim'pjeθa] : clear up **34**
limpio, ia ['limpjo, ja] adj. : clean **15**
locomotora [lokomo'tora] n. f. : engine **22**
lucir *[lu'θir] v. : shine* **73**
luna ['luna] n. f. : moon **66**
luz [luθ] n. f. : light

LL

llave ['ʎaβe] n. f. : key **9**
llegada [ʎe'ɣaða] n. f. : arrival **72**; finish **84**
lleno, na ['ʎeno, na] adj. : full **30**
llevar [ʎe'βar] v. : hold* **35**; wear* **39, 46**
llevar retraso [ʎe'βaṝe'traso] : be* late **22**
llover *[ʎo'βer] v. : rain **52**
lluvia ['ʎuβja] n. f. : rain **52, 67**

M

madre ['maðre] n. f. : mother **34, 35**
maduro, ra [ma'ðuro, ra] adj. : ripe **53**
maestro, tra [ma'estro, tra] n. : schoolteacher
mágico, ca ['maxiko, ka] adj. : magic **52**
malabarista [malaβa'rista] n. : juggler **93**
maleta [ma'leta] n. f. : suitcase **22**
mancha ['mantʃa] n. f. : stain **77**
mano ['mano] n. f. : hand **47**
manta ['manta] n. f. : blanket **12**
mantel [man'tel] n. m. : tablecloth **56**
mantequilla [mante'kiʎa] n. f. : butter **55**
manzana [man'θana] n. f. : apple **53**
mañana [ma'ɲana] n. f. : morning **52, 62**
mañana [ma'ɲana] adv. : tomorrow **31**, **52**
mapamundi [mapa'mundi] n. m. : globe **30**
mar [mar] n. m. : sea **65**
marcar [mar'kar] v. : show* **31**
marchito, ta [mar'tʃito, ta] adj. : wilted **63**
margarita [marɣa'rita] n. f. : daisy **63**
marido [ma'riðo] n. m. : husband **34**
mariposa [mari'posa] n. f. : butterfly **85**
marrón [ma'ṝon] adj. m. inv. : brown **29**
masajista [masa'xista] n. : masseur, euse **47**
medalla [me'ðaʎa] n. f. : medal **84**
media hora [me'ðja'ora] f. : half an hour **35**
medicina [meði'θina] n. f. : medicine **14, 49**
médico ['meðiko] n. m. : doctor **49**
medios de transporte ['meðjosdetrans'porte m. pl. : transport **23**
mejilla [me'xiʎa] n. f. : cheek **48**
mejor [me'xor] adj. : best **29**
mejor [me'xor] adv. : better **72**
melocotón [meloko'ton] n. m. : peach **53**
merienda de cumpleaños [me'rjendadekumple'aɲos] f. : birthday party **92**
mermelada [merme'laða] n. f. : jam **55**
mes [mes] n. m. : month **93**
mesa ['mesa] n. f. : table **54**
mesilla [me'siʎa] n. f. : bedside table **12**
micrófono [mi'krofono] n. m. : microphone **7**
tener* miedo [te'ner'mjeðo] : be* afraid **10, 69**
miel [mjel] n. f. : honey **55**

raya [ˈraǰa] n. f. : stripe 29
realmente [real'mente] adv. : really 55
rebajas [re'βaxas] n. f. pl. : sale 31
recreo [re'kreo] n. m. : playtime 27
rectángulo [rek'taŋgulo] n. m. : rectangle 30
redondo, da [re'ðondo, da] adj. : round 30
red [reθ] n. f. : net 86
red para coger mariposas
    [reθparako'xermari'posas] m. : butterfly net 85
regadera [reɣa'ðera] n. f. : watering can 8
regalo [re'ɣalo] n. m. : present 90, 92
regar* [re'ɣar] v. : water 8
regla [ˈreɣla] n. f. : ruler 77
relámpago [re'lampaɣo] n. m. : lightning 67
reloj [re'lox] n. m. : clock 22; watch 31, 48
reloj de cuco [re'loxde'kuko] m. : cuckoo
    clock 31
rellenar [reʎe'nar] v. : stuff 20
relleno [re'ʎeno] n. m. : stuffing 20
respirar [respi'rar] v. : breathe 49
resta [ˈresta] n. f. : subtraction 28
llevar retraso [ʎe'βarre'traso] : be* late 22
retrato [re'trato] n. m. : portrait 77
revisor [reβi'sor] n. m. : ticket collector 22
rico, ca [ˈriko, ka] adj. : rich 38
río [ˈrio] n. m. : river 64
rodar* [ro'ðar] v. : roll 43
rodilla [ro'ðiʎa] n. f. : knee 47
rojo, ja [ˈroxo, xa] adj. : red 29
rompecabezas [rompeka'βeθas] n. m. inv. :
    puzzle 75
romper* [rom'per] v. : break* 14
ropa [ˈropa] n. f. : clothes n. pl. 39, 40, 41
rosa [ˈrosa] n. f. : rose 63
rosa [ˈrosa] adj. m. inv. : pink 29
rubí [ru'βi] n. m. : ruby 43
rubio, ia [ˈruβjo, ja] adj. : blond, blonde 37

S

sábana [ˈsaβana] n. f. : sheet 12
saber* [sa'βer] v. : know* 29, 41, 60
sacar una foto [sa'karuna'foto] : take* a photo
    46, 91
saco de dormir [ˈsakodedor'mir] m. : sleeping
    bag 74
sal [sal] n. f. : salt 54
sala de juego [ˈsalade'xweɣo] f. : playroom 75
salida [sa'liða] n. f. : departure 72
salón [sa'lon] n. m. : sitting-room 69; drawing
    room 93
saltar [sal'tar] v. : jump 76, 84
salud [sa'luð] n. f. : health 49
salvaje [sal'βaxe] adj. : wild 69
sandalia [san'dalja] n. f. : sandal 47
sartén [sar'ten] n. f. : frying pan 57
saxofón [sa(ɣ)so'fon] n. m. : saxophone 79
tener* sed [te'nerseð] : be* thirsty 54, 81
segundo [se'ɣundo] n. m. : second 31
segundo, da [se'ɣundo, da] adj. : second 93
seguro, ra [se'ɣuro, ra] adj. : sure 20
sello [se'ʎo] n. m. : stamp 21
semáforo [se'maforo] n. m. : (traffic) light 18
semana [se'mana] n. f. : week 28
estar* sentado, da [es'tarsen'taðo, ða] : be*
    sitting down 11
sentirlo* mucho [sen'tirlo'mutʃo] : be* sorry 38
señal de tráfico [se'ɲalde'trafiko] f. : road
    sign 23
señor [se'ɲor] n. m. : gentleman 23
señora [se'ɲora] n. f. : lady 23, 46; woman 22, 72
ser* [ser] v. : be* 35
serpiente [ser'pjente] n. f. : snake 69
servilleta [serβi'ʎeta] n. f. : napkin 54
seta [ˈseta] n. f. : mushroom 60
seto [ˈseto] n. m. : hedge 8
siempre [ˈsjempre] adv. : always 29
siglo [ˈsiɣlo] n. m. : century 93
silla [ˈsiʎa] n. f. : chair 54

sillón [si'ʎon] n. m. : armchair 11
sintetizador [sinteti θa'ðor] n. m. : synthesizer 79
sobrina [so'brina] n. f. : niece 37
sobrino [so'βrino] n. m. : nephew 55, 92
¡socorro! [so'koro] interj. : help! 72
sol [sol] n. m. : sun 62, 73
sólido, da [ˈsoliðo, ða] adj. : sturdy 64
solución [solu'θjon] n. f. : solution 55
sombrero [som'brero] n. m. : hat 40, 80
sonámbulo, la [so'nambulo, la] n. :
    sleepwalker 57
sonar* [so'nar] v. : ring* 12, 31
sonreir* [sonre'ir] v. : smile 91
sopa [ˈsopa] n. f. : soup 57
sopera [so'pera] n. f. : soup tureen 57
soplar [so'plar] v. : blow* 65, 92
soportar [sopor'tar] v. : stand* 42
sorprendente [sorpren'dente] adj. : amazing 69
sorpresa [sor'presa] n. f. : surprise 14, 38
sortija [sor'tixa] n. f. : ring 43
sucio, ia [su'θjo, ja] adj. : dirty 15
suelo [ˈswelo] n. m. : floor 10, 43
en el suelo [enel'swelo] : on the ground 27
suerte [ˈswerte] n. f. : luck 31
suma [ˈsuma] n. f. : addition 28
supermercado [supermer'kaðo] n. m. :
    supermarket 20

T

tablero de juego de damas
    [ta'βlerode'xweɣode'damas] m. : draught-
    board 75
taburete [taβu'rete] n. m. : stool 14
tacón [ta'kon] n. m. : heel 42
tal vez [tal'beθ] adv. : perhaps 49
tallo [ˈtaʎo] n. m. : stem 63
también [tam'bjen] adv. : too 75
tarde [ˈtarðe] adv. : late 13, 29
tarta [ˈtarta] n. f. : tart 56
taxi [ˈta(ɣ)si] n. m. : taxi 23
taza [ˈtaθa] n. f. : cup 55
té [te] n. m. : tea 55
tejado [te'xaðo] n. m. : roof 9, 68
tejano [te'xano] n. m. : jeans n. pl. 40
tela [ˈtela] n. f. : canvas 77
teléfono [te'lefono] n. m. : telephone 11
llamar por teléfono [ʎa'marporte'lefono] :
    make* a telephone call 19
televisión [teleβi'sjon] n. f. : television 11
temprano [tem'prano] adv. : early 62
tenedor [tene'ðor] n. m. : fork 54
tener* hambre [te'ner'ambre] : be* hungry 54
tener* miedo [te'ner'mjeðo] : be* afraid 10, 69
tener* sed [te'nerseð] : be* thirsty 54, 81
tenis [ˈtenis] n. m. : tennis shoe 42
tenis de mesa [ˈtenisde'mesa] m. : table tennis 86
ternero [ter'nero] n. m. : calf 62
tetera [te'tera] n. f. : teapot 55
tía [ˈtia] n. f. : aunt 34
tiempo [ˈtjempo] n. m. : weather 67
tienda [ˈtjenda] n. f. : shop 20
tienda de campaña [ˈtjendadekam'paɲa] f. :
    tent 74
tienda de ultramarinos
    [ˈtjendade'ultrama'rinos] f. : grocer's shop 20
tintero [tin'tero] n. m. : inkwell 30
tío [ˈtio] n. m. : uncle 14, 34
tirar [ti'rar] v. : throw* 87
toalla [to'aʎa] n. f. : towel 15
tobogán [toβo'ɣan] n. m. : slide 81
tocar [to'kar] v. : play 78
tocar el claxon [to'karel'klaɣson] : hoot 19
tomar un baño [to'marun'baɲo] : have* a bath 15
tomate [to'mate] n. m. : tomato 91
torero [to'rero] n. m. : bullfighter 40
tormenta [tor'menta] n. f. : storm 67
torrente [to'rente] n. m. : mountain stream 61
tortilla [tor'tiʎa] n. f. : omelet 60

total [to'tal] n. m. : total 28
trabajar bien [traβa'xarbjen] : work hard 26
trabajo [tra'βaxo] n. m. : work 52; job 29
tráfico [ˈtrafiko] n. m. : traffic 19
traje [ˈtraxe] n. m. : suit 39, 41
traje de baño [ˈtraxede'baɲo] m. : bathing suit 7?
tren [tren] n. m. : train 22
trenza [ˈtrenθa] n. f. : plait 37
triángulo [trj'angulo] n. m. : triangle 30
trompeta [trom'peta] n. f. : trumpet 78
tronco [ˈtroŋko] n. m. : trunk 60
trueno [ˈtrweno] n. m. : thunder 67
tubo de pintura [ˈtuβodepin'tura] m. : tube of
    paint 77
tulipán [tuli'pan] n. m. : tulip 63
estar* tumbado, da [es'tartum'baðo, ða] : be*
    lying down 47

U

uva [ˈuβa] n. f. : grape 53

V

vacaciones [baka'θjones] n. f. pl. : holidays
    n. pl. 22, 73
vaca [ˈbaka] n. f. : cow 62
vaciar [ba'θjar] v. : empty 57
vacío, ía [ba'θio, ia] adj. : empty 30
vagón [ba'ɣon] n. m. : carriage 22
valle [ˈbaʎe] n. m. : valley 61
vaso [ˈbaso] n. m. : glass 14, 54
vela [ˈbela] n. f. : candle 92; sail 65
veleta [be'leta] n. f. : weathercock 68
vencedor, ra [benθe'ðor, ra] n. : winner 84
vendedor, ra [bende'ðor, ra] n. : salesperson 21
vender [ben'der] v. : sell* 9, 21
ventana [ben'tana] n. f. : window 9
ver* [ber] v. : see* 34, 46, 52, 53, 56, 67, 76, 80
verano [be'rano] n. m. : summer 73
verdaderamente [berða'ðeramente] adv. :
    really 77
verdadero, ra [berða'ðero, ra] adj. : real 57, 6?
verde [ˈberðe] adj. : green 18, 29
vestido [bes'tiðo] n. m. : dress 39
vestirse* [bes'tirse] v. : get* dressed 40
vía [ˈbia] n. f. : track 22
viejo, ja [ˈbjexo, xa] adj. : old 36
viento [ˈbjento] n. m. : wind 65
vientre [ˈbjentre] n. m. : stomach 46
vigilar [bixi'lar] v. : watch (over) 27; guard 68
violín [bjo'lin] n. m. : violin 78
vivir [bi'βir] v. : live 9
volar* [bo'lar] v. : fly* 62
volver* [bol'βer] v. : come* back 64
vuelta [ˈbwelta] n. f. : change 21

W

walkie-talkie [valki'talki] n. m. : walkie-talkie 6?

Y

yogur [ʝ(dʒ)o'ɣur] n. m. : yogurt 56

Z

zanahoria [θana'orja] n. f. : carrot 52
zapatilla [θapa'tiʎa] n. f. : slipper 41
zapato [θa'pato] n. m. : shoe 42, 67
zumo [ˈθumo] n. m. : juice 92

English – Spanish

A

:tor, tress ['æktə', tris] *n.* : actor, triz **80**
dition [ə'dɪʃ(ə)n] *n.* : suma *n. f.* **28**
dmire [əd'maɪə'] *v.* : admirar **90**
roplane ['ɛərəpleɪn] *n.* : avión *n. m.* **66, 72**
afraid [bɪə'freɪd] : tener* miedo **10, 69**
r hostess [ɛə'houstɪs] *f.* : azafata *n. f.* **72**
rport ['ɛəpɔːt] *n.* : aeropuerto *n. m.* **72**
sle [aɪsl] *n.* : pasillo *n. m.* **80**
arm clock [ə'lɑːmklɔk] : despertador *n. m.* **12, 31**
lot [ə'lɔt] *adv.* : mucho **56, 86**
lot (of) [ə'lɔt(ɒv)] : mucho, cha **41**
ways ['ɔːlwəz, -wɪz] *adv.* : siempre **29**
nazing [ə'meɪzɪŋ] *adj.* : sorprendente **69**
nbulance ['æmbjuləns] *n.* : ambulancia *n. f.* **49**
chor ['æŋkə'] *n.* : ancla *n. f.* **65**
gry ['æŋgri] *adj.* : furioso, sa **57**
aimal ['ænɪm(ə)l] *n.* : animal *n. m.* **68, 69, 76**
kle boot ['æŋk(ə)lbuːt] *n.* : botín *n. m.* **42**
norak ['ænəræk] *n.* : anorak *n. m.* **87**
t [ænt] *n.* : hormiga *n. f.* **91**
pearance [ə'pɪərəns] *n.* : aspecto físico *m.* **36**
pearances [ə'pɪərənsiz] *n. pl.* : apariencias *n. f. pl.* **27**
ple [æpl] *n.* : manzana *n. f.* **53**
ithmetic [ə'riθmətɪk] *n.* : cálculo *n. m.* **28**
'm [ɑːm] *n.* : brazo *n. m.* **35, 47**
'mchair ['ɑːmtʃɛə'] *n.* : sillón *n. m.* **11**
'rival [ə'raɪv(ə)l] *n.* : llegada *n. f.* **72**
'tist ['ɑːtɪst] *n.* : artista **77**
k for directions [ɑːskfɔː'd(a)i'rekʃ(ə)ns] : preguntar su camino **18**
l* asleep [fɔːlə'sliːp] *v.* : dormirse* **62**
hlete ['æθliːt] *n.* : atleta **84**
last [æt'lɑːst] *adv.* : por fin **30, 62**
idience ['ɔːdjəns] *n.* : público *n. m.* **78**
nt [ɑːnt] *n. f.* : tía **34**
itumn ['ɔːtəm] *n.* : otoño *n. m.* **60**

B

aby ['beibi] *n.* : nene, na **35, 48**
abysitter ['beibisitə'] *n.* : "canguro" **37**
ack [bæk] *n.* : espalda *n. f.* **46**; patio *n. m.* **93**
aker ['beikə'] *n.* : panadero, ra **20**
akery ['beikəri] *n.* : panadería *n. f.* **20**
alcony ['bælkəni] *n.* : balcón *n. m.* **9**
all [bɔːl] *n.* : pelota *n. f.* **75, 86**; balón *n. m.* **85**; bola *n. f.* **90**
anana [bə'nɑːnə] *n.* : plátano *n. m.* **53**
ank [bæŋk] *n.* : orilla *n. f.* **64**
ank note ['bæŋknout] : billete *n. m.* **21**
annisters ['bænistəz] *n. pl.* : barandilla *n. f.* **10**
arometer [bə'rɒmitə'] *n.* : barómetro *n. m.* **67**
asket ['bɑːskit] *n.* : cesta *n. f.* **91**
at [bæt] *n.* : raqueta *n. f.* **86**
ath [bɑːθ] *n.* : bañera *n. f.* **15**
ave* a bath [[hævə'bɑːθ] : tomar un baño **15**
athing suit [beiθiŋs(j)uːt] : traje de baño *m.* **73**

bathrobe ['bɑːθroub] *n.* : albornoz *n. m.* **15**
bathroom ['bɑːθruːm] *n.* : cuarto de baño *m.* **15**
be* [biː] *v.* : ser* **35**; estar* **21, 85**
beach [biːtʃ] *n.* : playa *n. f.* **73**
beach umbrella [biːtʃʌm'brelə] : quitasol *n. m.* **73**
bead [biːd] *n.* : perla *n. f.* **43**
bear ['bɛə'] *n.* : oso *n. m.* **30, 38**
beard [biəd] *n.* : barba *n. f.* **37**
beautiful ['bjuːtif(u)l] *adj.* : hermoso, sa **62**; bonito **93**
bed [bed] *n.* : cama *n. f.* **13**
bedroom ['bedru(:)m] *n.* : habitación *n. f.* **12**
bedside table ['bedsaidteibl] : mesilla *n. f.* **12**
bee [biː] *n.* : abeja *n. f.* **63**
be* hungry [biː'hʌŋgri] : tener* hambre **54**
be* late [biː'leit] : llevar retraso : **22**
believe [bi'liːv] *v.* : creer* **9**
belt [belt] *n.* : cinturón *n. m.* **41**
bench [ben(t)ʃ] *n.* : banco *n. m.* **81**
be* out of work [biːautɔːv'wəːk] : estar* en el paro **36**
best [best] *adj.* : mejor **29**
bet* [bet] *v.* : apostarse* **52**
be* thirsty [biː'θəːsti] : tener* sed **54, 81**
better ['betə'] *adv.* : mejor **72**
bicycle ['baisikl] *n.* : bicicleta *n. f.* **18**
big [big] *adj.* : grande **42**; ancho, cha **40**
bike [baik] *n.* : bici *n. f.* **19**
bird [bəːd] *n.* : pájaro *n. m.* **61, 62**
birthday ['bəːθdei] *n.* : cumpleaños *n. m. inv.* **92**
birthday party ['bəːθdei'pɑːti] : merienda de cumpleaños *f.* **92**
black [blæk] *adj.* : negro, gra **29**
blackboard ['blækbɔːd] *n.* : pizarra *n. f.* **26**
blanket ['blæŋkit] *n.* : manta *n. f.* **12**
blond, blonde [blɔnd] *adj.* : rubio, ia **37**
blouse [blauz] *n.* : blusa *n. f.* **39**
blow* ['blou] *v.* : soplar **65, 92**
blue [bluː] *adj.* : azul **29**
boat [bout] *n.* : barco *n. m.* **65**
body ['bɔdi] *n.* : cuerpo *n. m.* **46, 47**
bone [boun] *n.* : hueso *n. m.* **54**
book [buk] *n.* : libro *n. m.* **11, 27, 30**
boot [buːt] *n.* : bota *n. f.* **42**
bottle ['bɔtl] *n.* : botella *n. f.* **56**
bottom ['bɔtəm] *n.* : nalgas *n. f. pl.* **46**
bouquet [bu'kei] *n.* : ramo *n. m.* **63**
bow tie [boutai] : corbata de pajarita *f.* **39**
boy [bɔi] *n. m.* : muchacho **35**
bracelet ['breislit] *n.* : pulsera *n. f.* **43**
branch [brɑːn(t)ʃ] *n.* : rama *n. f.* **60**
bread [bred] *n.* : pan *n. m.* **55**
break* [breik] *v.* : romper* **14**
breakfast ['brekfəst] *n.* : desayuno *n. m.* **55**
breast [brest] *n.* : ala *n. f.* **90**
breathe [briːθ] *v.* : respirar **49**
bridge [bridʒ] *n.* : puente *n. m.* **64**
brooch [broutʃ] *n.* : broche *n. m.* **43**
brook [bruk] *n.* : arroyo *n. m.* **62**
brown [braun] *adj.* : marrón *adj. m. inv.* **29**
brush one's teeth [brʌʃwʌnstiːθ] : cepillarse los dientes **15**
build* [bild] *v.* : construir **64**

building ['bildiŋ] *n.* : edificio *n. m.* **18**
building block ['bildiŋblɔk] : cubo *n. m.* **75**
bullfighter [bulfaitə'] *n.* : torero *n. m.* **40**
bus [bʌs] *n.* : autobús *n. m.* **23**
bus fare [bʌsfɛər] : billete de autobús *m.* **28**
bus stop [bʌsstɔp] : parada del autobús *f.* **23**
butcher ['bʌtʃə'] *n.* : carnicero, ra **20**
butcher's shop ['bʌtʃəsʃɔp] : carnicería *n. f.* **20**
butter ['bʌtə'] *n.* : mantequilla *n. f.* **55**
butterfly ['bʌtəflai] *n.* : mariposa *n. f.* **85**
butterfly net ['bʌtəflainet] : red para coger mariposas *m.* **85**
buy* [bai] *v.* : comprar **9, 21, 52**
bye ! [bai] *interj.* : ¡ hasta luego ! **14**; ¡ hasta la vista ! **8**

C

cabbage ['kæbidʒ] *n.* : col *n. f.* **52**
cage [keidʒ] *n.* : jaula *n. f.* **93**
cake [keik] *n.* : pastel *n. m.* **14, 92**
calf *pl.* **calves** [kɑːf, kɑːvz] *n.* : ternero *n. m.* **62**
camel ['kæm(ə)l] *n.* : camello *n. m.* **76**
camera ['kæm(ə)rə] *n.* : cámara fotográfica *f.* **91**
camp [kæmp] *v.* : ir* de camping **74**
camping ['kæmpiŋ] *n.* : camping *n. m.* **74**
camping car ['kæmpiŋkɑː'] : autocar de camping *m.* **74**
can* [kæn] *v.* : poder* **80**
candle ['kænd(ə)l] *n.* : vela *n. f.* **92**
canoe [kə'nuː] *n.* : canoa *n. f.* **64**
canvas ['kænvəs] *n.* : tela *n. f.* **77**
cap [kæp] *n.* : gorro *n. m.* **41**; gorra *n. f.* **40**
car [kɑː'] *n.* : coche *n. m.* **18, 19**
caravan ['kærəvæn] *n.* : caravana *n. f.* **74**
carnation [kɑː'neiʃ(ə)n] *n.* : clavel *n. m.* **63**
car park [kɑː'pɑːk] : aparcamiento *n. m.* **18**
carriage ['kæridʒ] *n.* : vagón *n. m.* **22**
carrot ['kærət] *n.* : zanahoria *n. f.* **52**
cashier [kæ'ʃiə'] *n.* : cajero, ra **21**
cash register [kæʃ'redʒistə'] : caja *n. f.* **21**
cat [kæt] *n.* : gato, ta **68**
catch* [kætʃ] *v.* : coger* **76**; pescar **64**
cause [kɔːz] *v.* : provocar **19**
century ['sentjuri] *n.* : siglo *n. m.* **93**
cereal ['siəriəl] *n.* : cereales *n. m. pl.* **55**
chair [tʃɛə'] *n.* : silla *n. f.* **54**
chalet ['ʃælei] *n.* : chalet *n. m.* **61**
chamois ['ʃæmwɑː] *n.* : gamuza *n. f.* **61**
champion ['tʃæmpiən] *n.* : campeón, na **84**
change [tʃein(d)ʒ] *n.* : vuelta *n. f.* **21**
change [tʃein(d)ʒ] *v.* : cambiar **79**
cheap [tʃiːp] *adj.* : barato, ta **21**
check [tʃek] *v.* : comprobar* **20**
checkers ['tʃekəz] *n. pl.* : juego de damas *m.* **75**
cheek [tʃiːk] *n.* : mejilla *n. f.* **48**
cheese [tʃiːz] *n.* : queso *n. m.* **56**
cherry ['tʃeri] *n.* : cereza *n. f.* **53**
chess [tʃes] *n.* : ajedrez *n. m.* **75**
chestnut ['tʃes(t)nʌt] *n.* : castaña *n. f.* **60**
chicken ['tʃikin] *n.* : pollo *n. m.* **20, 56, 91**
chief [tʃiːf] *n.* : jefe *n. m.* **38**

child *pl.* **children** [tʃaild, 'tʃildrən] *n.* : niño, ña **27**; hijo, hija **35**

chimney ['tʃimni] *n.* : chimenea *n. f.* **9**

chin [tʃin] *n.* : barbilla *n. f.* **48**

chocolate ['tʃɔklət] *n.* : chocolate *n. m.* **92**

choose* [tʃuːz] *v.* : escoger* **69**

Christmas ['krisməs] *n.* : Navidad *n. f.* **90**

cinema ['sinəmə] *n.* : cine *n. m.* **80**

circle ['səːk(ə)l] *n.* : círculo *n. m.* **30**

circus ['səːkəs] *n.* : circo *n. m.* **93**

clap [klæp] *v.* : aplaudir **78**

class [klɑs] *n.* : clase *n. f.* **26**

classroom ['klɑːsruːm] *n.* : aula *n. f.* **26**

clean [kliːn] *adj.* : limpio, ia **15**

clean up [kliːnʌp] *v.* : hacer* la limpieza **34**

clearing [kliəriŋ] *n.* : claro del bosque *m.* **60**

clock [klɔk] *n.* : reloj *n. m.* **22**

close* [klouz] *v.* : cerrar* **84**

closed [klouzd] *adj.* : cerrado, da **9, 20, 30**

clothes [klouðz] *n. pl.* : ropa *n. f.* **39, 40, 41**

cloud [klaud] *n.* : nube *n. f.* **66**

clown [klaun] *n.* : payaso *n. m.* **93**

coat [kout] *n.* : abrigo *n. m.* **40**

coatstand [kout'stænd] *n.* : percha *n. f.* **40**

cock [kɔk] *n.* : gallo *n. m.* **68**

coffee ['kɔfi] *n.* : café *n. m.* **55**

coffee-pot ['kɔfipɔt] *n.* : cafetera *n. f.* **55**

coin [kɔin] *n.* : moneda *n. f.* **21**

cold [kould] *adj.* : frío, fría **74, 87, 91**

colour ['kʌləʳ] *n.* : color *n. m.* **29**

comb [koum] *n.* : peine *n. m.* **15**

come* **back** [kʌmbæk] *v.* : volver* **64**

comfortable ['kʌmfətəbl] *adj.* : cómodo, da **11**

competition [kɔmpi'tiʃ(ə)n] *n.* : concurso *n. m.* **79**

concentrate [kɔnsəntreit] *v.* : concentrarse **84**

concert ['kɔnsət] *n.* : concierto *n. m.* **78, 79**

conductor [kən'dʌktəʳ] *n.* : director de orquesta *m.* **78**

cook [kuk] *v.* : cocinar **14**

cooker ['kukəʳ] *n.* : cocina *n. f.* **14**

counter ['kauntəʳ] *n.* : mostrador *n. m.* **21**

country(side) ['kʌntri(said)] *n.* : campo *n. m.* **62**

court shoe [kɔːtʃuː] : escarpín *n. m.* **42**

cousin ['kʌz(ə)n] *n.* : primo, ma **34, 36**

cow [kau] *n.* : vaca *n. f.* **62**

cream [kriːm] *n.* : nata *n. f.* **14**

crocodile ['krɔkədail] *n.* : cocodrilo *n. m.* **69**

cross (the street) [krɔs(θəstriːt)] *v.* : cruzar* (la calle) **18, 19**

crossroads ['krɔsroudz] *n. pl.* : cruce *n. m.* **18**

cuckoo clock ['kuku:klɔk] : reloj de cuco *m.* **31**

cup [kʌp] *n.* : taza *n. f.* **55**

cupboard ['kʌbəd] *n.* : armario empotrado *m.* **14**

customs ['kʌstəms] *n. pl.* : aduana *n. f.* **72**

customs officer ['kʌstəms'ɔfisəʳ] *n.* : aduanero, ra **72**

cut* [kʌt] *v.* : cortar **35**

D

dance [dɑːns] *n.* : baile *n. m.* **39**

dance [dɑːns] *v.* : bailar **79**

dangerous ['dein(d)ʒ(ə)rəs] *adj.* : peligroso, sa **62, 85**

dark [dɑːk] *adj.* : oscuro, ra **10, 29**; moreno, na **37**

daughter ['dɔːtəʳ] *n. f.* : hija **34**

day [dei] *n.* : día **68**

decide [di'said] *v.* : decidir **68**

deep [diːp] *adj.* : profundo, da **64**

deer ['diəʳ] *n. inv.* : corzo *n. m.*

delicious [di'liʃəs] *adj.* : delicioso, sa **56, 60**

departure [di'pɑːtjəʳ] *n.* : salida *n. f.* **72**

desk [desk] *n.* : despacho *n. m.* **26**

die* [dai] *v.* : morir* **49**

dinner ['dinəʳ] *n.* : cena *n. f.* **57**

diploma [di'ploumə] *n.* : diploma *n. m.* **47**

direction [d(a)i'rekʃ(ə)n] *n.* : dirección *n. f.* **23**

---

dirty ['dəːti] *adj.* : sucio, ia **15**

dish [diʃ] *n.* : fuente *n. f.* **54**; plato *n. m.* **56**

do* **the dishes** [duːðədiʃiz] : fregar los platos **14**

division [di'viʒ(ə)n] *n.* : división *n. f.* **28**

doctor ['dɔktəʳ] *n.* : médico *n. m.* **49**

dog [dɔg] *n.* : perro, rra **68**

doll [dɔl] *n.* : muñeca *n. f.* **9, 75**

dollar ['dɔləʳ] *n.* : dólar *n. m.* **28, 47**

domino ['dɔminou] *n.* : dominó *n. m.* **75**

door [dɔːʳ] *n.* : puerta *n. f.* **9**

draught-board [drɑːftbɔːd] *n.* : tablero de juego de damas **75**

drawer ['drɔːəʳ] *n.* : cajón *n. m.* **41**

drawing room ['drɔːiŋruːm] : salón *n. m.* **93**

dress [dres] *n.* : vestido *n. m.* **39**

dressing gown ['dresiŋgaun] : bata *n. f.* **13**

drink* [driŋk] *v.* : beber **55**

drive* [draiv] *v.* : conducir* **23, 62**

drive* **mad** [draivmæd] : poner* nervioso, sa **11**

driver ['draivəʳ] *n.* : conductor, ra **23**

drums [drʌms] *n. pl.* : batería *n. f.* **79**

duck [dʌk] *n.* : pato *n. m.* **68**

dustbin ['dʌs(t)bin] *n.* : cubo de la basura *m.* **14**

dynamite ['dainəmait] *n.* : dinamita *n. f.* **19**

E

eagle ['iːgl] *n.* : águila *n. f.* **60, 61**

ear ['iəʳ] *n.* : oreja *n. f.* **48**

early ['əːli] *adv.* : temprano **62**

earring ['iːəriŋ] *n.* : pendiente *n. m.* **43**

eat* [iːt] *v.* : comer **54, 56, 60, 77, 92**

egg [eg] *n.* : huevo *n. m.* **55, 60, 61**

eiderdown ['aidədaun] *n.* : edredón *n. m.* **13**

elbow ['elbou] *n.* : codo *n. m.* **47**

electric [i'lektrik] *adj.* : eléctrico, ca **79**

elephant ['elifənt] *n.* : elefante *n. m.* **69**

emerald ['em(ə)rəld] *n.* : esmeralda *n. f.* **43**

empty ['em(p)ti] *adj.* : vacío, ía **30**

empty ['em(p)ti] *v.* : vaciar **57**

end [end] *n.* : final *n. m.* **93**

engine ['endʒin] *n.* : locomotora *n. f.* **22**

enthrall [in'θrɔːl] *v.* : cautivar **80**

excellent ['eksələnt] *adj.* : excelente **26**

exercise book ['eksəsaizbuk] : cuaderno *n. m.* **28**

expensive [eks'pensiv] *adj.* : caro, ra **21, 77**

explain [eks'plein] *v.* : explicar* **63**

explanation [eksplə'neiʃ(ə)n] *n.* : explicación *n. f.* **65**

eye [ai] *n.* : ojo *n. m.* **48, 84**

eyebrow ['aibrau] *n.* : pestaña *n. f.* **48**

eyelash ['ailæʃ] *n.* : ceja *n. f.* **48**

F

face [feis] *n.* : cara *n. f.* **48**

faithful ['feiθf(u)l] *adj.* : fiel **68**

fall* [fɔːl] *v.* : caer* **60, 87**

fall* **asleep** [fɔːlə'sliːp] *v.* : dormirse* **62**

family ['fæm(i)li] *n.* : familia *n. f.* **34**

famous ['feiməs] *adj.* : famoso, sa **38**

farm [fɑːm] *n.* : granja *n. f.* **68**

farmer ['fɑːməʳ] *n.* : granjero, ra **68**

fat [fæt] *adj.* : gordo, da **36**

father ['fɑːðəʳ] *n. m.* : padre **34**

fence [fens] *n.* : cercado *n. m.* **62**

fertilizer ['fəːtilaizəʳ] *n.* : abono *n. m.* **52**

fight* **back** [faitbæk] *v.* : defenderse **80**

figure ['figəʳ] *n.* : cifra *n. f.* **28**

film [film] *n.* : película *n. f.* **80**

find* [faind] *v.* : encontrar* **39, 60, 61**

finger ['fiŋgəʳ] *n.* : dedo *n. m.* **47**

finish ['finiʃ] *n.* : llegada *n. f.* **84**

fire ['faiəʳ] *n.* : fuego *n. m.* **74**

fireplace ['faiəpleis] *n.* : chimenea *n. f.* **90**

fir tree [fəːʳtriː] : abeto *n. m.* **64**

---

first [fəːst] *adj.* : primero, primer, primera **40, 9**

first of all [fəːstɔvɔːl] *adv.* : primero **92**

fish *pl.* **fishes** [fiʃ, 'fiʃiz] *n.* : pez *n. m.* **64, 76**; pescado *n. m.* **57**

fish bowl [fiʃboul] : acuario *n. m.* **11**

fisherman *pl.* **-men** ['fiʃəmæn, -men] *n. m.* : pescador, ra **64**

fishing rod ['fiʃiŋrɔd] : caña de pescar *f.* **64**

flat [flæt] *n.* : apartamento *n. m.* **93**

floor [flɔːʳ] *n.* : suelo *n. m.* **10, 43**; piso *n. m.* **93**

florist ['flɔrist] *n.* : florista. **63**

flow [flou] *v.* : fluir* **64**

flower ['flauəʳ] *n.* : flor *n. f.* **8, 63**

flute [fluːt] *n.* : flauta *n. f.* **78**

fly* [flai] *v.* : volar* **62**

flying saucer [flaiŋ'sɔːsəʳ] : platillo volante *m.* **6**

fog [fɔg] *n.* : niebla *n. f.* **62**

food [fuːd] *n.* : comida *n. f.* **51**

foot *pl.* **feet** [fut, fiːt] *n.* : pie *n. m.* **42, 47**

forbidden [fə'bidn] *adj.* : prohibido, do **18**

forehead ['fɔrid, 'fɔːhed] *n.* : frente *n. f.* **48**

forest ['fɔrist] *n.* : bosque *n. m.* **60**

forget* [fə'get] *v.* : olvidar **22, 41, 84**

fork [fɔːk] *n.* : tenedor *n. m.* **54**

fountain ['fauntin] *n.* : fuente *n. f.* **81**

fridge [fridʒ] *n.* : nevera *n. f.* **57**

friend [frend] *n.* : amigo, ga **27**

fringe [frindʒ] *n.* : flequillo *n. m.* **37**

frown [fraun] *v.* : fruncir el ceño **46**

fruit [fruːt] *n.* : fruta *n. f.* **53**

frying pan ['fraiŋpæn] : sartén *n. f.* **57**

full [ful] *adj.* : lleno, na **30**

have* **fun** [hævfʌn] : divertirse* **27, 42, 75**

G

game [geim] *n.* : juego *n. m.* **75**; partida *n. f.* **75** partido *n. m.* **86**

garage ['gærɑːʒ] *n.* : garaje *n. m.* **9**

garden ['gɑːd(ə)n] *n.* : jardín *n. m.* **8, 69**

garland ['gɑːlənd] *n.* : guirnalda *n. f.* **90**

gentleman *pl.* **-men** ['dʒent(ə)lmæn, -men] *n. m.* : señor **23**

get* **changed** [get'tʃein(d)ʒd] : cambiarse de ropa **92**

get* **dressed** [get'dresd] *v.* : vestirse* **40**

get* **up** [getʌp] *v.* : levantarse **12**

giraffe [dʒi'ræf, -'rɑːf] *n.* : jirafa *n. f.* **69, 76**

girl [gəːl] *n. f.* : niña **23, 35, 37**; chica **39**

give* [giv] *v.* : dar* **92**

glad [glæd] *adj.* : contento, ta **74**

glass [glɑːs] *n.* : vaso *n. m.* **14, 54**

glasses [glɑːsiz] *n. pl.* : gafas *n. f. pl.* **46**

glitter ['glitəʳ] *v.* : brillar **43**

globe [gloub] *n.* : mapamundi *n. m.* **30**

go* [gou] *v.* : ir* **20, 39, 57, 76**

goat [gout] *n.* : cabra *n. f.* **62**

gold [gould] *n.* : oro *n. m.* **43**

goldfish ['gouldfiʃ] *n.* : pez *n. m.* **11**

good [gud] *adj.* : bueno, buen, buena **29, 79**

go* **to bed** [goutuːbed] : irse* a acostar **75**

grandfather ['græn(d)fɑːðəʳ] *n. m.* : abuelo **34**

grandmother ['græn(d)mʌðəʳ] *n. f.* : abuela **3**

grape [greip] *n.* : uva *n. f.* **53**

grass [grɑːs] *n.* : hierba *n. f.* **60**

green [griːn] *adj.* : verde **18, 29**

green bean [griːnbiːn] : judía verde *f.* **52**

grey [grei] *adj.* : gris **29**

grill [gril] *v.* : asar **74**

grocer's shop ['grousəzʃɔp] : tienda de ultramarinos *f.* **20**

on the **ground** [ɔnθəgraund] : en el suelo **27**

grow* [grou] *v.* : crecer* **52**

guard [gɑːd] *v.* : vigilar **68**

guest [gest] *n.* : invitado, da **40**; convidado, da **9**

guitar [gi'tɑːʳ] *n.* : guitarra *n. f.* **74, 79**

gym [dʒim] *n.* : gimnasio *n. m.* **85**

gymnastics [dʒim'næstiks] *n. pl.* : gimnasia *n. f.* **85**

H

air ['hɛər] n. : pelo n. m. 35, 48; cabellos n. m. pl. 37
alf an hour ['hɑ:fən'auər] : media hora f. 35
all [hɔ:l] n. : pasillo n. m. 10
and [hænd] n. : mano n. f. 47; aguja n. f. 31
and basin [hænd'beis(ə)n] : lavabo n. m. 15
angar ['hæŋər] n. : hangar n. m. 72
ang*up [hæŋʌp] v. : colgar* 67
appen ['hæp(ə)n] v. : pasar 76
appy ['hæpi] adj. : feliz 35; contento, ta 30, 31, 38; alegre 15
arbour ['hɑ:bər] n. : puerto n. m. 65
arp [hɑ:p] n. : arpa n. f. 79
at [hæt] n. : sombrero n. m. 40, 80
ead [hed] n. : cabeza n. f. 46
ave*a bath [[hævə'bɑ:θ] : tomar un baño 15
ave*a headache [hævə'hedeik] : dolerle* a uno la cabeza 49
ave*fun [hævfʌn] : divertirse* 27, 42, 75
ead [hed] n. : cabeza n. f. 46
eadlight ['hedlait] n. : faro n. m. 19
eadmaster [hed'mɑ:stər] n. m. : director, ra 26
ealth [helθ] n. : salud n. f. 49
eart [hɑ:t] n. : corazón n. m. 49
eavy ['hevi] adj. : pesado, da 22
ectic ['hektik] adj. : agitado, da 66
edge [hedʒ] n. : seto n. m. 8
eel [hi:l] n. : tacón n. m. 42
elp [help] n. : ayuda n. f. 26
elp! [help] interj. : ¡ socorro ! 72
elp [help] v. : ayudar 28, 87
en [hen] n. : gallina n. f. 68
enhouse ['henhaus] n. : gallinero n. m. 68
ero ['hiərou] n. : héroe n. m. 80
ide* ['haid] v. : esconderse 76
ppopotamus pl. -muses, -mi [hipə'pɔtəməs, -məsiz, -mai] n. : hipopótamo n. m. 69
old* ['hould] v. : llevar 35
oliday ['hɔlidei] n. : fiesta n. f. 89
olidays ['hɔlideiz] n. pl. : vacaciones n. f. pl. 22, 73
omework ['houmwərk] n. : deberes n. m. pl. 28
oney ['hʌni] n. : miel n. f. 55
oot [hu:t] v. : tocar el claxon 19
ope [houp] v. : esperar 29
orse [hɔ:s] n. : caballo n. m. 68
ospital ['hɔspit(ə)l] n. : hospital n. m. 49
our ['auər] n. : hora n. f. 31, 35
ouse [haus] n. : casa n. f. 7, 9, 10, 67, 68
uman ['hju:m(ə)n] adj. : humano, na 45
e*hungry [bi:'hʌngri] : tener* hambre 54
unt [hʌnt] v. : cazar 38
urry ['hʌri] v. : darse* prisa 93
usband ['hʌzbənd] n. m. : marido 34

I

e cream ['aiskri:m] : helado n. m. 92
ea [ai'diə] n. : idea n. f. 66, 68
mpossible [im'pɔsibl] adj. : imposible 9
ndian ['indiən] n. : Indio, ia 64
ndian ['indiən] adj. : indio, ia 38
fluence ['influəns] n. : influencia n. f. 26
jection [in'dʒekʃ(ə)n] n. : inyección n. f. 49
kwell ['iŋkwel] n. : tintero n. m. 30
strument ['instrumənt] n. : instrumento n. m. 79
vitation [invi'teiʃ(ə)n] n. : invitación n. f. 92
vite [in'vait] v. : invitar 38

J

cket ['dʒækit] n. : chaqueta n. f. 39; americana n. f. 40
m [dʒæm] n. : mermelada n. f. 55

jeans [dʒi:nz] n. pl. : tejano n. m. 40
jetty ['dʒeti] n. : escollera n. f. 65
jewellery ['dʒu:əlri] n. : joyas n. f. pl. 43
job [dʒɔb] n. : trabajo n. m. 29
juggler ['dʒʌglər] n. : malabarista 93
juice [dʒu:s] n. : zumo n. m. 92
jump [dʒʌmp] v. : saltar 76, 84

K

kangaroo [kæŋgə'ru:] n. : canguro n. m. 76
keep*one's mouth shut [ki:pwʌnsmauθʃʌt] : callarse 38
kennel ['ken(ə)l] n. : casilla n. f. 68
key [ki:] n. : llave n. f. 9
kilo ['ki:lou] n. : kilo n. m. 20
kitchen ['kitʃin] n. : cocina n. f. 14, 57
kite [kait] n. : cometa n. f. 66, 91
knee [ni:] n. : rodilla n. f. 47
knife pl. knives [naif, naivz] n. : cuchillo n. m. 54
know* [nou] v. : saber* 29, 41, 60

L

ladle ['leidl] n. : cucharón n. m. 57
lady ['leidi] n. f. : señora 23, 46
lamp [læmp] n. : lámpara n. f. 12
land [lænd] v. : aterrizar* 72
landscape ['læn(d)skeip] n. : paisaje n. m. 62
late [leit] adv. : tarde 13, 29
be*late [bi:leit] : llevar retraso : 22
lawn [lɔ:n] n. : césped n. m. 8
lawn mower ['lɔ:nmouər] : cortacésped n. m. 8
leaf pl. leaves [li:f, li:vz] n. : hoja n. f. 60
learn* [lə:n] v. : aprender 27, 30
leave* [li:v] v. : dejar 54
leek [li:k] n. : puerro n. m. 52
leg [leg] n. : pierna n. f. 47; muslo n. m. 90; pata n. f. 56
leisure ['leʒər] n. : ocio n. m. 71
lemonade [lemə'neid] n. : gaseosa n. f. 92
let* [let] v. : dejar 13
lettuce ['letis] n. : lechuga n. f. 52
light [lait] n. : luz n. f. 10
light [lait] adj. : claro, ra 29
(traffic) light [('træfik)lait] n. : semáforo n. m. 18
lighthouse ['laithaus] n. : faro n. m. 65
lightning ['laitniŋ] n. : relámpago n. m. 67
like [laik] v. : gustarle a uno 57
lion ['laiən] n. : león, na 69
listen ['lis(ə)n] v. : escuchar 30
live [liv] v. : vivir 9
lock [lɔk] n. : cerradura n. f. 9
log [lɔg] n. : leño n. m. 90
lollipop ['lɔlipɔp] n. : pirulí n. m. 92
long [lɔŋ] adj. : largo, ga 37, 69
look after [luk'ɑ:ftər] v. : cuidar 49
look for [lukfɔ:r] v. : buscar 93
lorry ['lɔri] n. : camión n. m. 23
love [lʌv] v. : querer* 8
lovely ['lʌvli] adj. : hermoso, sa 53; bonito, ta 9, 31, 39
luck [lʌk] n. : suerte n. f. 31
luggage ['lʌgidʒ] n. : equipaje n. m. 22
lunch [lʌn(t)ʃ] n. : almuerzo n. m. 56
be*lying down [bi:laiŋdaun] : estar* tumbado, da 47

M

magic ['mædʒik] adj. : mágico, ca 52
man pl. men [mæn, men] n. m. : hombre 35
marble ['mɑ:bl] n. : canica n. f. 27

masseur, euse [mæ'sər, mæ'sə:z] n. : masajista 47
masterpiece ['mɑ:stəpi:s] n. : obra maestra f. 77
mattress ['mætris] n. : colchón n. m. 12
meadow ['medou] n. : pradera n. f. 62
meal [mi:l] n. : comida n. f. 91
meat [mi:t] n. : carne n. f. 56, 74
medal ['med(ə)l] n. : medalla n. f. 84
medicine ['med(i)sin] n. : medicina n. f. 14, 49
mess [mes] n. : desorden n. m. 34
microphone ['maikrəfoun] n. : micrófono n. m. 79
milk [milk] n. : leche n. f. 21, 55
minute ['minit] n. : minuto n. m. 31
mirror ['mirər] n. : espejo n. m. 15
make*a mistake [meikəmis'teik] : equivocarse 28
mobile ['moubail] n. : móvil n. m. 75
money ['mʌni] n. : dinero n. m. 21
monkey [mʌŋki] n. : mono n. m. 69
month [mʌnθ] n. : mes 93
moon [mu:n] n. : luna n. f. 66
morning ['mɔ:niŋ] n. : mañana n. f. 52, 62
moth [mɔθ] n. : polilla n. f. 41
mother ['mʌðər] n. f. : madre 34, 35
motorcycle ['moutəsaikl] n. : moto n. f. 23
mountain ['mauntin] n. : montaña n. f. 61
mountain stream ['mauntinstri:m] : torrente n. m. 61
moustache [məs'tɑ:ʃ] n. : bigote n. m. 37
mouth [mauθ] n. : boca n. f. 48
multiplication [mʌltipli'keiʃ(ə)n] n. : multiplicación n. f. 28
muscled ['mʌsld] adj. : musculoso, sa 47
museum [mju(:)'ziəm] n. : museo n. m. 61
mushroom ['mʌʃrum] n. : seta n. f. 60
music ['mju:zik] n. : música n. f. 78, 79
musician [mju'ziʃ(ə)n] n. : músico, ca 79

N

napkin ['næpkin] n. : servilleta n. f. 54
narrow ['nærou] adj. : estrecho, cha 10
nature ['neitjər] n. : naturaleza n. f. 59
neck [nek] n. : cuello n. m. 46, 69
necklace ['neklis] n. : collar n. m. 43
need [ni:d] v. : necesitar 36
nephew ['nefju] n. m. : sobrino n. m. 55, 92
nest [nest] n. : nido n. m. 60
net [net] n. : red n. f. 86
new [nju:] adj. : nuevo, va 39, 69
nice [nais] adj. : amable 38
niece [ni:s] n. f. : sobrina n. f. 37
night [nait] n. : noche n. f. 66
nightcap ['naitkæp] n. : gorro de dormir m. 13
nose [nouz] n. : nariz n. f. 48
now [nau] adv. : ahora 66, 72, 92
nurse [nə:s] n. : enfermera n. f. 49

O

okay ! ['ou'kei] interj. : ¡ de acuerdo ! 92
old [ould] adj. : viejo, ja 36
omelet ['ɔmlit] n. : tortilla n. f. 60
onion ['ʌnjən] n. : cebolla n. f. 52
open ['oup(ə)n] adj. : abierto, ta 30
open ['oup(ə)n] v. : abrir* 84
orange ['ɔrin(d)ʒ] n. : naranja n. f. 53, 92
orange ['ɔrin(d)ʒ] adj. : naranja adj. m. inv. 29
orchestra ['ɔ:kistrə] n. : orquesta n. f. 78
ostrich ['ɔ:striʃ] n. : avestruz n. m. 76
other ['ʌðər] adj. : otro, tra 76
be*out of work [bi:autɔv'wə:k] : estar* en el paro 36
oven ['ʌv(ə)n] n. : horno n. m. 14
owl [aul] n. : lechuza n. f. 66

P

page [peidʒ] n. : página n. f. 26
paint [peint] v. : pintar 77
paint brush [peint'brʌʃ] : pincel n. m. 77
painting ['peintiŋ] n. : pintura n. f. 77; cuadro n. m. 77, 93
palette ['pælit] n. : paleta n. f. 77
palm tree [pɑːmtriː] : palmera n. f. 73
paper [peipəʳ] n. : papel n. m. 77
paper ['peipəʳ] v. : empapelar 69
parade [pə'reid] v. : desfilar 93
parcel ['pɑːs(ə)l] n. : paquete n. m. 19
park [pɑːk] n. : parque n. m. 81
park [pɑːk] v. : aparcar 18
part [pɑːt] n. : parte n. f. 47
birthday **party** ['bə:θdei'pɑːti] : merienda de cumpleaños f. 92
passenger ['pæsəndʒəʳ] n. : pasajero, ra 23
passport ['pɑːspɔːt] n. : pasaporte n. m. 72
path [pɑːθ] n. : alameda n. f. 8
pavement ['peivmənt] n. : acera n. f. 18
pay* [pei] v. : pagar* 21
pea [piː] n. : guisante n. m. 52
peach [piːtʃ] n. : melocotón n. m. 53
peak [piːk] n. : cumbre n. f. 61
pear ['pɛəʳ] n. : pera n. f. 53
pebble [pebl] n. : guijarro n. m. 64
pedestrian [pi'destriən] n. : peatón n. m. 19
peg [peg] n. : perchero n. m. 41
pen [pen] n. : bolígrafo n. m. 28
pencil ['pens(ə)l] n. : lápiz n. m. 77
penguin ['peŋgwin] n. : pingüino n. m. 76
people ['piːpl] n. : gente n. f. 33
pepper ['pepəʳ] n. : pimienta n. f. 54
performance [pə'fɔːməns] n. : espectáculo n. m. 93
performer [pə'fɔːməʳ] n. : artista 93
perhaps [pə'hæps, præps] adv. : tal vez 49
personality [pəːsə'næliti] n. : personalidad n. f. 38
petal [pet(ə)l] n. : pétalo n. m. 63
petticoat ['petikout] n. : enaguas n. f. pl. 39
photo ['foutou] n. : foto n. f. 46, 91
take* a **photo** [teikə'foutou] : sacar una foto 46, 91
piano [pi'ænou] n. : piano n. m. 78
pick up ['pikʌp] v. : ir* a buscar 37
picnic ['piknik] n. : picnic n. m. 91
pig [pig] n. : cerdo n. m. 62, 68
pillow [pilou] n. : almohada n. f. 13
pineapple ['painæpl] n. : piña n. f. 53
pink [piŋk] adj. : rosa adj. m. inv. 29
plait [plæt] n. : trenza n. f. 37
plane [plein] n. : avión n. m. 72
plant [plɑːnt] n. : planta n. f. 52, 63
plant [plɑːnt] v. : plantar 8
green **plant** [griːn'plɑːnt] : planta de interior f. 63
plate [pleit] n. : plato n. m. 14, 54
platform ['plætfɔːm] n. : andén n. m. 22
play [plei] v. : jugar* 27, 75, 85, 86; tocar 78
player ['pleiəʳ] n. : jugador, ora 86
playground ['pleigraund] n. : patio n. m. 27
playroom ['pleiruːm] n. : sala de juego f. 75
playtime ['pleitaim] n. : recreo n. m. 27
pocket money ['pɔkit'mʌni] : propina n. f. 28
podium pl. -dia ['poudiəm, -diə] n. : podio n. m. 84
police [pə'liːs] n. : policía n. f. 65
policeman pl. -men [p(ə)'liːsmæn, -men] n. m. : policía 18
polite [pə'lait] adj. : bien educado, da 38
pond [pɔnd] n. : charca n. f. 68
ponytail ['pouniteil] n. : cola de caballo f. 37
poor [puəʳ] adj. : pobre 38, 77
portrait ['pɔːtreit] n. : retrato n. m. 77
postman pl. -men ['poustmæn, -men] n. m. : cartero 18
post office [poust'ɔfis] : correos n. m. pl. 18
potato [p(ə)'teitou] n. : patata n. f. 52
practical ['præktik(ə)l] adj. : práctico, ca 55

Q

present ['prezənt] n. : regalo 90, 92
price [prais] n. : precio n. m. 9
projector [prə'dʒektəʳ] n. : proyector n. m. 80
puddle ['pʌdl] n. : charco n. m. 67
pullover ['pulouvəʳ] n. : jersey n. m. 41
pumpkin ['pʌmpkin] n. : calabaza n. f. 52
pupil ['pjuːp(i)l] n. : alumno, na 26
purple ['pəːpl] adj. : morado, da 29
purse [pəːs] n. : monedero n. m. 21
puschair [pʌstʃɛəʳ] n. : cochecito n. m. 81
put* [put] v. : poner* 27
puzzle ['pʌzl] n. : rompecabezas n. m. inv. 75
pyjamas [pə'dʒɑːməs] n. pl. : pijama n. m. 13

question ['kwestʃ(ə)n] n. : pregunta n. f. 27
quickly ['kwikli] adv. : deprisa 69

R

rabbit ['ræbit] n. : conejo n. m. 62
race [reis] n. : carrera n. f. 84
radish ['rædiʃ] n. : rábano n. m. 52
rain [rein] n. : lluvia n. f. 52, 67
rain [rein] v. : llover* 52
raincoat ['reinkout] n. : impermeable n. m. 40, 67
raise [reiz] n. : aumento n. m. 28
rake [reik] n. : rastrillo n. m. 8
read* [riːd] v. : leer* 11
real ['riəl] adj. : verdadero, ra 57, 64
really ['riəli] adv. : verdaderamente 77; realmente 55
record [ri'kɔːd] n. : disco n. m. 37
rectangle ['rektæŋgl] n. : rectángulo n. m. 30
red [red] adj. : rojo, ja 29
red-haired ['red'hɛəd] adj. : pelirrojo, ja 37
rent [rent] v. : alquilar 9, 93
rice [rais] n. : arroz n. m. 56
rich [ritʃ] adj. : rico, ca 38
ride* a **horse** [raidə'hɔːs] : montar a caballo 68
rider ['raidəʳ] n. : caballista n. m. 93
ring [riŋ] n. : sortija n. f. 43; anillo n. m. 43; pista n. f. 93
ring* [riŋ] v. : sonar* 12, 31
ripe [raip] adj. : maduro, ra 53
river ['rivəʳ] n. : río n. m. 64
road sign [roudsain] : señal de tráfico f. 23
roll [roul] v. : rodar* 43
roller skate ['roulə'skeit] : patín de ruedas m. 85
roof [ruːf] n. : tejado n. m. 9, 68
rose [rouz] n. : rosa n. f. 63
round [raund] adj. : redondo, da 30
rubber ['rʌbəʳ] n. : goma n. f. 77
rubber ring ['rʌbə'riŋ] : boya n. f. 73
ruby ['ruːbi] n. : rubí n. m. 43
rucksack ['rʌksæk] n. : mochila n. f. 74
rug [rʌg] n. : alfombra n. f. 12
ruler ['ruːləʳ] n. : regla n. f. 77
run* [rʌn] v. : correr 27, 69, 84
runway ['rʌnwei] n. : pista n. f. 72

S

sail [seil] n. : vela n. f. 65
sale [seil] n. : rebajas n. f. pl. 31
salesperson [seilz'pəːs(ə)n] n. : vendedor, ra 21
salt [sɔlt] n. : sal n. f. 54
sand [sænd] n. : arena n. f. 73
sandal ['sænd(ə)l] n. : sandalia n. f. 47
sand castle [sændkɑːs(ə)l] : castillo de arena m. 73
sandwich ['sændwitʃ] n. : bocadillo n. m. 91
satchel ['sætʃ(ə)l] n. : cartera n. f. 28

saucepan ['sɔːspən] n. : cazuela n. f. 14
saxophone ['sæksəfoun] n. : saxofón n. m. 79
say* [sei] v. : decir* 42
school [skuːl] n. : escuela n. f. 25, 26, 27, 30
schoolteacher ['skuːltiːtʃəʳ] n. : maestro, tra 2
scream [skriːm] v. : chillar 80
screen [skriːn] n. : pantalla n. f. 80
sea [siː] n. : mar n. m. 65
seagull ['siːgʌl] n. : gaviota n. f. 66
seat [siːt] n. : butaca n. f. 80
second ['sekənd] n. : segundo n. m. 31
second ['sekənd] adj. : segundo, da 93
see* [siː] v. : ver* 34, 46, 52, 53, 56, 67, 76, 80
see you soon! [siːjusuːn] interj. : ¡ hasta pronto 8, 22
sell* [sel] v. : vender 9, 21
shampoo [ʃæm'puː] n. : champú n. m. 15
shape [ʃeip] n. : forma n. f. 30
sheet [ʃiːt] n. : sábana n. f. 12
shelf pl. shelves [ʃelf, ʃelvz] n. : estantería n. f. 14
shell [ʃel] n. : concha n. f. 73
shelter ['ʃeltəʳ] v. : ponerse* a cubierto 67
shine* [ʃain] v. : brillar 66; lucir* 73
ship [ʃip] n. : buque n. m. 65
shirt [ʃəːt] n. : camisa n. f. 41
shoe [ʃuː] n. : zapato n. m. 42, 67
shoelace ['ʃuːleis] n. : cordón n. m. 42
shoes [ʃuːz] n. pl. : calzado n. m. 42
shop [ʃɔp] n. : tienda n. f. 20
shop [ʃɔp] v. : ir* de compras 20
short [ʃɔːt] adj. : corto, ta 37, 40
shorts [ʃɔːts] n. pl. : pantalón corto m. 85
shoulder ['ʃouldəʳ] n. : hombro n. m. 46
shovel ['ʃʌv(ə)l] n. : pala n. f. 8
show* [ʃou] v. : presentar 72; marcar 31
show* the way [ʃouðə'wei] : indicar* el camino 18
shutter ['ʃʌtəʳ] n. : contraventana n. f. 9
sick [sik] adj. : enfermo, ma 49
singer ['siŋəʳ] n. : cantante 79
sing* out of tune [siŋautɔvtjuːn] : desafinar 7
sink [siŋk] n. : fregadero n. m. 14
sink* [siŋk] v. : hundirse 64
be* sitting down [biːsitiŋdaun] : estar* sentado, da : 11
sitting-room ['sitiŋruː(ː)m] n. : salón n. m. 69; cuarto de estar m. 11
skate board ['skeitbɔːd] : monopatín n. m. 85
ski [skiː] n. : esquí n. m. 87
ski [skiː] v. : esquiar 87
ski hat [skihæt] : gorro n. m. 87
skiing [skiiŋ] n. : esquí n. m. 87
skirt [skəːt] n. : falda n. f. 40
sky [skai] n. : cielo n. m. 66
sleep* [sliːp] v. : dormir* 13, 74
sleeping bag ['sliːpiŋbæg] : saco de dormir m.
sleepwalker ['sliːpwɔːkəʳ] n. : sonámbulo, la
sleigh [slei] n. : pequeño trineo m. 87
slide [slaid] n. : tobogán n. m. 81; pasador n. m. 37
slide* [slaid] v. : deslizar 81
slipper ['slipəʳ] n. : zapatilla n. f. 41
slope [sloup] n. : pista n. f. 87
small [smɔːl] adj. : bajo, ja 36
smart [smɑːt] adj. : elegante 39
smile [smail] v. : sonreir* 91
smock [smɔk] n. : delantal n. m. 77
smoke [smouk] n. : humo n. m. 74
snake [sneik] n. : serpiente n. f. 69
snow [snou] n. : nieve n. f. 87
snow [snou] v. : nevar* 87
snowball ['snoubɔːl] n. : bola de nieve f. 87
snowman pl. -men [snoumæn, -men] n. m. : muñeco de nieve 87
soap [soup] n. : jabón n. m. 15
sock [sɔk] n. : calcetín n. m. 41
solution [sə'luːʃ(ə)n] n. : solución n. f. 55
son [sʌn] n. m. : hijo 34
soon [suːn] adv. : pronto 12
be* sorry [biː'sɔri] : sentirlo* mucho 38

oup [suːp] n. : sopa n. f. 57
oup tureen [suːptjuəˈriːn] : sopera n. f. 57
pectator [spekˈteitər] n. : espectador, ra 93
ponge [spʌn(d)ʒ] n. : esponja n. f. 14
poon [spuːn] n. : cuchara n. f. 54
port [spɔːt] n. : deporte n. m. 83
portsgear [spɔːtsgiər] n. : equipo n. m. 85
pring [spriŋ] n. : primavera n. f. 8
quare [ˈskwɛər] n. : cuadrado n. m. 30
quirrel [ˈskwir(ə)l] n. : ardilla n. f. 60
range squeezer [ˈɔrin(d)ʒˈskwiːzər] : exprimidor n. m. 36
tadium [ˈsteidiəm] n. : estadio n. m. 84
tag [stæg] n. : ciervo n. m. 76
tage [steidʒ] n. : escena n. f. 78
tain [stein] n. : mancha n. f. 77
tairs [ˈstəz] n. pl. : escalera n. f. 10
tamp [stæmp] n. : sello n. m. 21
tand* [stænd] v. : soportar 42
e* standing up [biːstændiŋʌp] : estar* de pie 47
tar [staːr] n. : estrella n. f. 66
tarch [staːtʃ] n. : almidón n. m. 87
tarving [ˈstaːviŋ] adj. : hambriento, ta 77
tation [ˈsteiʃ(ə)n] n. : estación n. f. 22
tem [stem] n. : tallo n. m. 63
tep [step] n. : escalón n. m. 10
tereo [ˈsteriou] n. : equipo estereofónico m. 11
tomach [ˈstʌmək] n. : vientre n. m. 46
tool [stuːl] n. : taburete n. m. 14
torm [stɔːm] n. : tormenta n. f. 67
traight [streit] adj. : lacio, ia 37
trange [strein(d)ʒ] adj. : extraño, ña 42
trawberry [ˈstrɔːb(ə)ri] n. : fresa n. f. 53
treet [striːt] n. : calle n. f. 18, 93
tripe [straip] n. : raya n. f. 29
trong [strɔŋ] adj. : fuerte 36, 85
tuff [stʌf] v. : rellenar 20
tuffing [ˈstʌfiŋ] n. : relleno n. m. 20
turdy [ˈstəːdi] adj. : sólido, da 64
ubtraction [səbˈtrækʃ(ə)n] n. : resta n. f. 28
ugar [ˈʃugər] n. : azúcar n. m. 21, 55
ugar dispenser [ˈʃugərdisˈpensər] : azucarero n. m. 55
uit [s(j)uːt] n. : traje n. m. 39, 41
uitcase [ˈs(j)uːtkeis] n. : maleta n. f. 22
ummer [ˈsʌmər] n. : verano n. m. 73
un [sʌn] n. : sol n. m. 62, 73
unglasses [ˈsʌnglaːsiz] n. pl. : gafas de sol f. pl. 73
un-tanned [ˈsʌntænd] adj. : moreno, na 73
upermarket [s(j)uːˈpəmaːkit] n. : supermercado n. m. 20
ure [ˈʃuər] adj. : seguro, ra 20
urprise [səˈpraiz] n. : sorpresa n. f. 14, 38
weet [swiːt] n. : caramelo n. m. 28, 92
weet pepper [swiːtˈpepər] : pimiento n. m. 52
wim* [swim] v. : nadar 65, 68
wing [swiŋ] n. : columpio n. m. 81
ynthesizer [ˈsinθəsaizər] n. : sintetizador n. m. 79
yringe [ˈsirindʒ, siˈrindʒ] n. : jeringuilla n. f. 49

T

able [ˈteibl] n. : mesa n. f. 54
ablecloth [ˈteiblklɔθ] n. : mantel n. m. 56
able tennis [ˈteiblˈtenis] : tenis de mesa m. 86
ake* a photo [teikəˈfoutou] : sacar una foto 46, 91
ake* off [ˈteikɔf] v. : despegar* 72
alk* [tɔːk] v. : hablar 76
all [tɔːl] adj. : alto, ta 36
amer [ˈteimər] n. : domador, ra 93
ap [tæp] n. : grifo n. m. 15
art [taːt] n. : tarta n. f. 56
axi [ˈtæksi] n. : taxi n. m. 23

tea [tiː] n. : té n. m. 55
teacher [ˈtiːtʃər] n. : profesor, ra 27
teapot [ˈtiːpɔt] n. : tetera n. f. 55
teddy bear [ˈtedibɛər] : oso de felpa m. 75
tee-shirt [ˈtiːʃəːt] n. : camiseta n. f. 41
telephone [ˈtelifoun] n. : teléfono n. m. 11
make* a telephone call [meikəˈtelifounkɔːl] : llamar por teléfono 19
telephone kiosk [ˈtelifounkiɔːsk] : cabina telefónica f. 19
television [teliˈviʒ(ə)n] n. : televisión n. f. 11
tell* [tel] v. : decir* 52
tennis shoe [ˈtenisʃuː] : tenis n. m. 42
tent [tent] n. : tienda de campaña f. 74
thanks ! [θæŋks] interj. : ¡ gracias ! 28, 36
thin [θin] adj. : delgado, da 36
think* [θiŋk] v. : pensar* 87; creer 35, 43
be* thirsty [biːˈθəːsti] : tener* sed 54, 81
throw* [θrou] v. : tirar 87
thunder [ˈθʌndər] n. : trueno n. m. 67
ticket collector [ˈtikitkəˈlektər] : revisor n. m. 22
tie [tai] n. : corbata n. f. 39
tights [taits] n. pl. : panty n. m. 39
time [taim] n. : hora n. f. 14, 31
tired [ˈtaid] adj. : cansado, da 13
today [təˈdei] adv. : hoy 27, 60, 72
toe [tou] n. : dedo del pie n. m. 47
tomato [təˈmaːtou] n. : tomate n. m. 91
tomorrow [təˈmɔrou] adv. : mañana 31, 52
tongue [tʌŋ] n. : lengua n. f. 48
tonight [təˈnait] adv. : esta noche 39
too [tuː] adv. : demasiado 40, 42, 62, 85; también 75
tooth pl. teeth [tuːθ, tiːθ] n. : diente n. m. 15, 48
toothbrush [ˈtuːθbrʌʃ] n. : cepillo de dientes m. 15
toothpaste [ˈtuːθpeist] n. : dentífrico n. m. 15
total [ˈtout(ə)l] n. : total n. m. 28
towel [ˈtauəl] n. : toalla n. f. 15
town [taun] n. : ciudad n. f. 17, 29
toy [tɔi] n. : juguete n. m. 75
track [træk] n. : vía n. f. 22; huella n. f. 30; pista n. f. 84; camino n. m. 23
tracksuit [ˈtræks(j)uːt] n. : chandal n. m. 85
traffic [ˈtræfik] n. : tráfico n. m. 19
traffic jam [ˈtræfikdʒæm] : atasco n. m. 18, 19
train [trein] n. : tren n. m. 22
transport [ˈtrænsːpɔːt] n. : medios de transporte m. pl. 23
tree [triː] n. : árbol n. m. 8, 60, 90
triangle [ˈtraiæŋgl] n. : triángulo n. m. 30
trousers [ˈtrauzəz] n. pl. : pantalón n. m. 40
trumpet [ˈtrʌmpit] n. : trompeta n. f. 78
trunk [trʌŋk] n. : tronco n. m. 60
try* [trai] v. : intentar 65
tube of paint [tjuːbɔvpeint] : tubo de pintura m. 77
tulip [ˈtjuːlip] n. : tulipán n. m. 63
turkey [ˈtəːki] n. : pavo n. m. 90
tyre [ˈtaiər] n. : neumático n. m. 19

U

ugly [ˈʌgli] adj. : feo, fea 36
umbrella [ʌmˈbrelə] n. : paraguas n. m. inv. 67
umpire [ˈʌmpaiər] n. : árbitro, tra 86
uncle [ˈʌŋkl] n. : tío n. m. 14, 34
understand* [ʌndəˈstænd] v. : entender* 30

V

valley [ˈvæli] n. : valle n. m. 61
vase [vaːz] n. : florero n. m. 11

vegetables [ˈvedʒ(i)təbls] n. pl. : hortalizas n. f. pl. 52
very [ˈveri] adv. : muy 39, 62
vest [vest] n. : camiseta n. f. 85
viewer [ˈvjuər] n. : espectador, ra 80
violin [vaiəˈlin] n. : violín n. m. 78

W

wait (for) [weit(fɔːr)] v. : esperar 23, 60, 62, 69, 92
wake* up [ˈweikʌp] v. : despertarse 12
walkie-talkie [wɔːkiˈtɔki] n. : walkie-talkie n. m. 61
wall [wɔːl] n. : pared n. f. 9
wallet [ˈwɔlit] n. : cartera n. f. 21
wallpaper [ˈwɔːlpeipər] n. : papel (pintado) n. m. 86
want [wɔnt] v. : querer* 20, 29, 53
wardrobe [ˈwɔːdroub] n. : armario n. m. 12; guardarropa n. m. 41
warm oneself [wɔːmwʌnˈself] v. : calentarse 74
wash oneself [wɔʃwʌnˈself] v. : lavarse 15
watch [wɔtʃ] n. : reloj n. m. 31, 48
watch (over) [wɔtʃ(ˈouvər)] v. : vigilar 27
watch television [wɔtʃteliˈviʒ(ə)n] : mirar la televisión : 11
water [ˈwɔːtər] n. : agua n. f. 57
water [ˈwɔːtər] v. : regar* 8
watering can [ˈwɔːtəriŋkæn] : regadera n. f. 8
water-ski* [ˈwɔːtərskiː] v. : hacer* esquí náutico 65
wear* [wɛər] v. : llevar 39, 46
weather [ˈweðər] n. : tiempo n. m. 67
weathercock [ˈweðəkɔk] n. : veleta n. f. 68
week [wiːk] n. : semana n. f. 28
weigh [wei] v. : pesar 20
weights [weits] n. pl. : pesas n. f. pl. 85
well [wel] adv. : bien 34, 77, 86
wet [wet] adj. : mojado, da 67
white [(h)wait] adj. : blanco, ca 29
wife pl. wives [waif, waivz] n. f. : mujer 34
wild [waild] adj. : salvaje 69
wilted [ˈwiltid] adj. : marchito, ta 63
win* [win] v. : ganar 84, 86
wind [wind] n. : viento n. m. 65
window [ˈwindou] n. : ventana n. f. 9
winner [ˈwinər] n. : vencedor, ra 84
winter [ˈwintər] n. : invierno n. m. 87
woman pl. -men [ˈwumən, -min] n. f. : mujer 35; señora 22, 72
wood [wud] n. : leña n. f. 74
work [wəːk] n. : trabajo n. m. 52
work hard [wəːkhaːd] : trabajar bien 26
worried [ˈwʌrid] adj. : preocupado, da 49
write* [rait] v. : escribir* 26

Y

yawn [jɔːn] v. : bostezar* 13
yellow [ˈjelou] adj. : amarillo, lla 29
yogurt [ˈjɔgət] n. : yogur n. m. 56
young [jʌŋ] adj. : joven 35

Z

zebra [ˈziːbrə] n. : cebra n. f. 69, 76
zebra crossing [ˈziːbrəkrɔsiŋ] : paso de peatones m. 23
zoo [zuː] n. : parque zoológico m. 76

Printed in Spain
by Graficromo, S.A. Córdoba